simple recipes
— FOR —
busy seasons

DEVOTIONAL COOKBOOK

Simple Recipes for Busy Seasons: Devotional Cookbook
Copyright © 2025 DaySpring. All rights reserved.
First Edition, September 2025

Published by:

21154 Highway 16 East
Siloam Springs, AR 72761
dayspring.com

All rights reserved. *Simple Recipes for Busy Seasons: Devotional Cookbook* is under copyright protection. No part of this book may be used or reproduced in any manner whatsoever without written permission except in the case of brief quotations embodied in critical articles and reviews.

Scripture quotations marked TLB are taken from The Living Bible copyright © 1971. Used by permission of Tyndale House Publishers, Inc., Carol Stream, Illinois 60188. All rights reserved.

Scripture quotations marked GNT are taken from the Good News Translation in Today's English Version-Second Edition Copyright © 1992 by American Bible Society. Used by Permission.

Scripture quotations marked NLT are taken from the Holy Bible, New Living Translation, copyright © 1996, 2004, 2007, 2015 by Tyndale House Foundation. Used by permission of Tyndale House Publishers, Inc., Carol Stream, Illinois 60188. All rights reserved.

Scripture quotations marked THE MESSAGE are taken from THE MESSAGE, copyright © 1993, 1994, 1995, 1996, 2000, 2001, 2002 by Eugene H. Peterson. Used by permission of NavPress. All rights reserved. Represented by Tyndale House Publishers, Inc.

Scripture quotations marked THE VOICE are taken from The Voice™. Copyright © 2008 by Ecclesia Bible Society. All rights reserved.

Scripture quotations marked NIV are taken from the Holy Bible, New International Version®, NIV®. Copyright © 1973, 1978, 1984, 2011 by Biblica, Inc.® Used by permission of Zondervan. All rights reserved worldwide. www.zondervan.com. The "NIV" and "New International Version" are trademarks registered in the United States Patent and Trademark Office by Biblica, Inc.®

Scripture quotations marked CSB® are taken from the Christian Standard Bible®, Copyright © 2017 by Holman Bible Publishers. Used by permission. Christian Standard Bible®, and CSB® are federally registered trademarks of Holman Bible Publishers.

Written by: Nancy Cockrell
Food Photography: Nancy Cockrell
Cover Design by: Becca Barnett

Printed in Vietnam
Prime: U4461
ISBN: 979-8-88603-376-2

contents

Introduction 9

SPRING 10

    Fresh Beginnings 12

    Spinach Artichoke Strata 14

    Nourish Your Soul 16

    Honey-Almond Granola 18

    Sweetly Spoken 20

    Easy Cheese Danish 22

    Grace upon Grace 24

    7-Layer Dip 26

    Spring Cleaning 28

    Bacon-Ranch Cheese Ball 30

    Refreshed and Renewed 32

    Refreshing Fruit Salad 34

    A Well-Watered Garden 36

    Easy Cobb Salad 38

    Incomparable 40

    Chicken Broccoli Rice Casserole 42

    Breathe In God's Goodness 44

    Easter Egg Blondies 46

    Filled Up 48

    Lemon-Filled Cupcakes 50

    Sweet and Simple 52

    Strawberry Crinkle Cookies 54

    The Changing Seasons: Spring-Summer 56

SUMMER 58

    A New Day and New Mercies 60

    Blueberry Chip Muffins 62

    Growing Strong Roots 64

    Cherry-Almond Coffee Cake 66

    Cultivating Contentment 68

    Veggie Crescent Pizza 70

    Life-Giving Light 72

    Berry Tarts 74

    Take a Break 76

    Stuffed Ranch Eggs 78

    He Cares and Provides 80

    Classic Potato Salad 82

    Never Stop Blooming 84

    Strawberry Spinach Salad 86

    Calm in the Storm 88

    Taco Pasta Salad 90

    True Freedom 92

    Easy Patriotic Cookies 94

    Beautifully Transformed 96

    Peach Cobbler Cake 98

    Living with Purpose 100

    Chocolate Mint Brownies 102

    The Changing Seasons: Summer-Fall 104

FALL 106

    Lessons from the Trees 108

    Apple-Cheddar Biscuits 110

    Enjoying Cozy Comforts 112

    Pumpkin Coffee Cake 114

    Lifelong Learning 116

    Apple Baked Oatmeal 118

    Harvesttime. 120

    Pumpkin Pecan Bread 122

    Your Cheering Section 124

    Loaded Baked Potato Dip 126

    Grateful Always 128

    Caramel Apple Dip 130

    Gathering Together 132

    Apple-Pear Salad. 134

    The Right Path 136

    Corn Casserole 138

    Bountiful Blessings 140

    Secret Ingredient Chili 142

    Traditions and Remembering. 144

    Chocolate Chip Coconut Oatmeal Cookies 146

    Embrace Each Season 148

    Mini Apple Bundt Cakes 150

    The Changing Seasons: Fall-Winter 152

WINTER 154

    Rest for Your Soul.. 156

    Cranberry Quick Bread... 158

    Good Gifts.. 160

    Crumb Coffee Cake... 162

    Looking Forward with Hope..................................... 164

    Apple-Cranberry Muffins.. 166

    Perfect Peace... 168

    Million Dollar Dip.. 170

    Great Joy.. 172

    Charcuterie Snack Board.. 174

    Perfect Love.. 176

    Loaded Baked Potato Soup..................................... 178

    A Warm Welcome... 180

    Creamy Cheesy Potatoes.. 182

    A Generous Heart.. 184

    Turkey Tetrazzini.. 186

    For His Glory... 188

    Graham Cracker Toffee.. 190

    Wait Patiently.. 192

    Ginger Shortbread Cookies..................................... 194

    Live in Wonder... 196

    Marshmallow Pops... 198

    The Changing Seasons: Winter-Spring......................... 200

Index.. 202

introduction

Spring, summer, fall, winter . . . the rhythm of the changing seasons each year is familiar and comforting, isn't it? Spring is a season of new beginnings, summer is a time of growth, fall is a time of harvest, and winter is a time of rest. Just as God has given every season in nature a purpose, He also has a purpose for the different seasons that we walk through in our own lives—seasons of new experiences and change, seasons of thriving, seasons of abundance, and seasons of challenges.

One of the blessings of the changing seasons is that there's always something to look forward to! We love the winter wonderland of snowy landscapes but are thankful the cold weather won't last forever. The warmer days of spring and blooming flowers aren't far behind! We may wish the lake and beach days of summer would last longer, but we love the crisp air and vibrant colors that fall brings. We enjoy decorating our homes to welcome the new seasons and find comfort in the familiarity of favorite traditions and foods our families enjoy. We plan for special holiday and church events, gatherings, and meals that make each season special. We look forward to spending time with family and friends as we come together in our homes and around the table.

But so often, we're pressed for time. There never seems to be enough of it! How will we get everything done in our already-busy days? In this book, you'll find encouraging devotions paired with coordinating recipes to nourish both your body and soul—a blend of spiritual reflection and simple, wholesome meals to bring peace and joy to your everyday life.

It is my hope that when you're feeling a little overwhelmed, whatever season you're in, this book will inspire you to draw close to God. That you'll see His blessing and care in every season and embrace all the beauty and goodness you discover around you. That you'll enjoy making (and eating) the simple, tasty recipes. And that your heart and home will be filled with peace and joy, even in the busiest of times!

Nancy

spring

The flowers are springing up and the time of the singing of birds has come. Yes, spring is here.

SONG OF SOLOMON 2:12 TLB

It seems like nature starts to awaken from a deep sleep when spring arrives. As the weather warms up, we notice signs of new life growing around us! Trees bud and blossom, tulips and daffodils start peeking up from beneath the earth, and we hear birds chirping as they get ready to build their nests.

Spring is a season of new beginnings—a beautiful reminder that God loves to do new things in our lives. It might be hard to see the "new" as we try to keep up with our daily routines and check off tasks on our to-do lists. But if we take time to be quiet, listen to His voice, and stay open to the good plans He has for us, we can see Him work in amazing ways!

Maybe He's planted a dream in your heart and He's calling you to move forward in faith to the next step. Maybe He wants you to do a "spring cleaning" in your life, letting go of some activities so you can have more "me" time. Or maybe it's time to move on to new things that are more life-giving for you. Whatever your "new thing" is, know that God is with you, leading the way and providing everything you need. Let this be a season of discovering the fresh, new things He wants to do in you and through you!

fresh beginnings

"Watch for the new thing I am going to do. It is happening already—you can see it now! I will make a road through the wilderness and give you streams of water there."

ISAIAH 43:19 GNT

Everything about spring feels so fresh and hopeful. Maybe that's why so many of us love this season! As we enjoy the new life springing up around us in nature, we also look forward to God doing something new in us. Are you at a place in your life where you're ready for a fresh start? Have you been ready for something new for a long time but feeling a little discouraged, thinking God has forgotten about you? Or maybe you're feeling stuck in a "wilderness season" where you're at right now—a little worn out and overwhelmed by responsibilities at home and work. And you're so ready for a fresh beginning.

The beautiful truth is that God loves to do new things in our lives, and He is always working things out for our good, even when it seems like nothing is happening. His timing may be very different from ours, but we can know without a doubt that His ways are so much better. This very moment, He is busy orchestrating the details of our lives into something better than we could ever imagine. And that "wilderness season" that you're so ready to be over with just might be helping to prepare you for the "something new" God has for you. We can be confident that in these challenging times, God doesn't waste anything that happens in our lives. He uses it all—even the hard stuff—to help us grow stronger in our faith, preparing us for the next new season.

So wait expectantly for God to bring about a fresh beginning in your life. He tells us, *Look! See! Watch for it! This new thing I'm doing in you is springing up. It's growing. It's sprouting. It's already beginning to happen!* Even if we're feeling stuck in the place where we are or we're a little fearful of change, we can move forward with the assurance that He is making a road through the wilderness. He is making a way even when there doesn't seem to be one—He is opening doors that need to be opened for us to walk through. He is smoothing and clearing out the paths we need to move forward on. And He is giving us streams of water to refresh us and revive us on our journey. We can trust that when God is leading us, He will equip us with everything we need for a fresh beginning.

Just as God equips us for new beginnings in life, starting your day with a nourishing and flavorful dish like Spinach-Artichoke Strata can set the tone for a fresh start. Spinach and artichokes are popular spring veggies and make a great flavor combination. There are some other vegetables in this strata, too, so it's filled with good things. As you chop the veggies and prepare them in the pan, think about God's goodness in your life and thank Him for the fresh beginnings He's given you—and the ones that are to come!

We are confident that God is able to orchestrate everything to work toward something good and beautiful when we love Him and accept His invitation to live according to His plan.
ROMANS 8:28 THE VOICE

Jesus replied, "My Father is always working, and so am I."
JOHN 5:17 NLT

God specializes in giving people a fresh start.
RICK WARREN

"For I know the plans I have for you," declares the Lord, "plans to prosper you and not to harm you, plans to give you hope and a future."
JEREMIAH 29:11 NIV

Morning by morning He wakens me and opens my understanding to His will.
ISAIAH 50:4 NLT

It is great to be faced with the impossible, for nothing is impossible if one is meant to do it. Wisdom will be given, and strength. When the Lord leads, He always strengthens.
AMY CARMICHAEL

spinach artichoke strata

You'll need to include time to refrigerate the strata mixture for an hour before baking it…or refrigerate it overnight and bake the strata in the morning.

PREP: 20 MIN. | COOK: 60 MIN. | TOTAL TIME: 80 MIN. | SERVINGS: 4–6

2 tablespoons olive oil

¾ cup onion, chopped (about 1 medium)

1 garlic clove, minced

¾ cup red bell pepper, chopped (about 1 medium)

6 cups fresh baby spinach leaves

1 (14-ounce) can quartered artichoke hearts, drained

5 cups crusty bread, cut into 1-inch cubes

2½ cups shredded Monterey Jack cheese, divided

5 large eggs

1½ cups milk

½ teaspoon salt

¼ teaspoon pepper

1. Preheat oven to 350°F. Grease a 2-quart baking dish; set aside.

2. In a large skillet, heat oil over medium heat. Add chopped onion, garlic, and red bell pepper, cooking for 4 minutes. Then add the spinach leaves and cook another 3 to 4 minutes, until spinach is wilted and everything else is tender. Remove skillet from heat. Stir in the artichoke hearts; set aside.

3. In a large bowl, combine the cubed bread, the onion/spinach mixture from the skillet, and 2 cups of the shredded cheese, tossing everything together well. Add mixture to the greased baking dish, spreading evenly.

4. In another bowl, beat the eggs, milk, salt, and pepper together. Pour this mixture over the bread mixture in the baking dish. Cover and refrigerate for at least an hour or overnight.

5. Cover with foil and bake at 350°F for 30 minutes, then uncover, sprinkle the top with the remaining 1/2 cup cheese, and bake uncovered 30 minutes longer, or until top is lightly browned and knife inserted in center comes out clean. Let cool for 10 minutes, then cut and serve.

nourish your soul

**Thrill to God's Word . . .
chew on Scripture day and night.
You're a tree replanted in Eden,
bearing fresh fruit every month,
never dropping a leaf, always in blossom.**
PSALM 1:2–3 THE MESSAGE

We all have those days when we get so busy running around, we don't have time to sit down and eat! In the morning, we might grab a cup of coffee and a donut in the drive-through, get some fast food for lunch (or maybe even skip lunch), and have no idea what we're going to make or buy for dinner. We might be able to do this eating-on-the-run routine for a while, but eventually it catches up with us and we start feeling tired, irritated, maybe even a little forgetful. We're just not at our best. On the other hand, when we eat nourishing foods, we feel and function better. Our bodies are better equipped to get through the day because we're not running on empty; we're filled with the nourishment we need to keep going.

Spiritual nourishment is a lot like physical nourishment. When we don't spend time in God's Word, we may feel drained, overwhelmed, and stressed. But when we are "chewing" and "feeding" on it, we are filling up on the kind of nourishment that restores our souls, renews our minds, gives us peace and strength, and helps us grow in our faith. Scripture calms us, comforts us, and helps us throughout our day.

When we are spiritually well-nourished by God's Word, we thrive and grow—we *bear fresh fruit* and are always *in blossom*. As we are chewing on Scripture and being filled with its goodness and truth, we can also better show the love and care of Jesus to others—by giving them a hug, providing a helping hand, or praying for them. Nourishing our souls is so important to living our best life—feeding on God's Word, growing closer to Him each day, and sharing His love and truth with others so they can be nourished too.

Just as we gain spiritual nourishment by feeding our souls with God's Word, we can also get physical nourishment by fueling our bodies with something wholesome like Honey-Almond Granola. It's great for breakfast as a cereal with milk, or you can make a breakfast parfait with it by generously sprinkling it over yogurt. As you prepare a simple breakfast with this granola, take some time to thank God for how He provides nourishment for both our bodies and our souls. He takes care of us so well!

*Lord, You are so good and gracious to us.
Thank You for blessing our lives in so many ways
and for giving us the precious gift of Your Word.
As we read it, our souls are nourished and filled with
peace. We know that You are right there with us,
speaking to our hearts. Your words are Living Water to
us, and we need them every day to grow and flourish.
Thank You for walking through the busyness of our
days with us and working everything out for our
good. And thank You for loving us so much—more
than we can comprehend. Help us to be faithful in
taking the time to be fed by Your Word and Your
presence every day. Be with us as we grow stronger
in our faith and in our obedience to what Your Word
teaches so we can live a life that glorifies You. Amen.*

honey-almond granola

For a simple breakfast, serve as a cereal with milk or sprinkle over yogurt.

PREP: 15 MIN. | COOK: 32 MIN. | TOTAL TIME: 47 MIN. | SERVINGS: 10–12

⅓ cup canola oil or light olive oil

½ cup honey

⅓ cup light brown sugar, packed

½ teaspoon salt

Optional: ½ teaspoon almond extract

4½ cups rolled oats

1 cup sliced almonds

1 cup golden raisins

1. Preheat oven to 325°F. Line a 13 x 18-inch rimmed baking sheet with parchment paper; set aside.

2. In a large bowl, mix together the oil, honey, brown sugar, salt, and almond extract (if using). Fold in the rolled oats and sliced almonds, mixing everything together well, making sure all the oats and almonds are coated.

3. Spread mixture evenly on lined baking sheet and bake for 28 to 32 minutes, until golden, stirring halfway through the baking time to help the granola bake evenly.

4. When finished baking, remove from oven and stir in the golden raisins while granola is still on baking sheet. Let it cool completely on pan (it will get crunchier as it cools).

5. After granola has cooled, stir again, breaking up any clumps, and serve it with milk as a cereal or sprinkle it over yogurt to make a breakfast parfait. It makes a great snack too. Store in an airtight container at room temperature for up to 2 weeks.

sweetly spoken

**Let everything you say be good and helpful,
so that your words will be an encouragement
to those who hear them.**

EPHESIANS 4:29 NLT

You've probably heard the phrase, "The best things in life are sweet." For some, that might mean sweet times with family and friends, sweet memories . . . or maybe even sweet things to eat! But even more special are the sweet, encouraging words people say to us, and the uplifting words we say to others. They're like little treasures we keep in our hearts.

Sometimes we don't pay much attention to the words we speak in our daily conversations, especially when we're in a hurry, and we probably don't realize how much of an impact they have. But they really can make a difference in the lives of those around us, whether we're talking to family, friends, or casual acquaintances. Kind and encouraging words are so powerful—they can be such a blessing to anyone we cross paths with. When we speak them, they can build others up and give them strength.

The Bible says kind words are sweet to our souls: "Kind words are like honey—sweet to the soul and healthy for the body" (Proverbs 16:24 NLT). Who doesn't feel uplifted when someone gives us a thoughtful compliment, an encouraging word, or a friendly "Great to see you!"? Or when someone stops to pray for us when we're going through a difficult time—that can bring such comfort! Those are sweet gifts we love to receive and can give to others. Not only are gracious words sweet to the soul, but they can also be healthy for the body. Speaking words of hope to someone can be soothing and reviving, helping to melt away stress and worry.

Words spoken with grace, love, kindness, and care are simple ways to make a big difference in someone's life. And sharing helpful truths from God's Word with others can be such an encouragement to them too. Let's ask God to give us the right words to share with whomever we see each day. We don't know who we may run into, but God does, and He knows their needs.

Maybe you've thought about spending some time with a friend or friends to catch up and encourage each other. Why not invite them over for coffee or tea and make something sweet and simple, like Easy Cheese Danish, to enjoy as you visit? When you mix the creamy filling for the Danish and slice the dough, take a little time to pray and think about how your words can bring encouragement and hope to your friends. The sweet words you speak may be exactly what their hearts need to hear!

*Encourage each other and build each other
up, just as you are already doing.*
1 THESSALONIANS 5:11 NLT

*A well-spoken word at just the right moment is
like golden apples in settings of silver.*
PROVERBS 25:11 THE VOICE

*Kind words do not cost much.
Yet they accomplish much.*
BLAISE PASCAL

*Let your conversation be always full of grace,
seasoned with salt, so that you
may know how to answer everyone.*
COLOSSIANS 4:6 NIV

*Pursue a life that creates peace
and builds up our brothers and sisters.*
ROMANS 14:19 THE VOICE

*Kind words can be short and easy to speak,
but their echoes are truly endless.*
MOTHER TERESA

easy cheese danish

*Get a sweet start to your day with this easy-to-make Danish.
If you want, you can add a little jam on top of the cream cheese
or sprinkle with chopped pecans before baking.*

PREP: 20 MIN. | COOK: 14 MIN. | TOTAL TIME: 34 MIN. | SERVINGS: 16

- 1 (8-ounce) package cream cheese, softened
- ½ cup powdered sugar
- ½ teaspoon pure vanilla extract
- 2 (8-ounce) cans refrigerated crescent rolls
- ¼ cup chopped nuts (pecans or walnuts)
- Glaze: Mix 3/4 cup powdered sugar with 1 to 1½ tablespoons milk.

1. Preheat oven to 375°F. Line 2 baking sheets with parchment paper; set aside.

2. In a medium-size bowl, with a large mixing spoon or hand mixer, mix the cream cheese, powdered sugar, and vanilla together; set aside.

3. Remove crescent roll dough from the packages, but keep the dough rolled up. Cut each roll of dough into 8 slices (for a total of 16 slices) with a serrated knife and place 2 inches apart on lined baking sheets.

4. Make an indention in each sliced round by pressing down with the bottom of a small jar (the size of a spice jar) dipped in flour to avoid sticking. After pressing down, the size of each round should be about 2½ inches.

5. Spoon a heaping ½ tablespoon of the cream cheese mixture into the center of each round, spreading mixture slightly.

6. Bake for 12 to 14 minutes, until golden. Cool on baking sheet for a few minutes, then place on a platter and let cool completely. After cooling, drizzle with glaze and sprinkle with nuts.

grace upon grace

**We have all received grace upon grace
from His fullness.**

JOHN 1:16 CSB

Ever feel like giving up when everything seems to be going wrong, or when there's so much to do and so little time? We've all felt that way! Like when we're worn out from driving to and from all those after-school activities and events. And when we're running behind on things at work and deadlines are looming. Or when we spend time helping or caring for friends or family who need our support. We may even be struggling physically with an illness, or struggling emotionally with a difficult relationship. It could be any number of things, and they can feel so overwhelming.

That's where God's grace comes in—His undeserved favor, love, and mercy. When we accept this gift of God's grace through Jesus, we see it unfold throughout our lives, grace upon grace, a never-ending supply. We see it in the challenging seasons—when He gives us the strength we need to get through a difficult day, when He gives us the wisdom we need to make important choices or decisions, or when He fills us with the peace we need to walk through a time of hardship or loss. His grace is abundant and always enough to meet our needs. The Lord tells Paul in II Corinthians 12:9 (THE VOICE): "My grace is enough to cover and sustain you. My power is made perfect in weakness." And Paul adds, in verse 10, "When I am at my weakest, He makes me strong." What a comfort that is! Nothing we face is too big for us to bring to God. He can handle it! And nothing is too small to bring to Him—He cares about every single detail of our lives. We can always know that when we ask Him, God will give us the power to do what we can't do in our own strength.

Many times, we may not see or understand how God is working, but like a bud in springtime that gradually unfolds petal by petal and blossoms into a beautiful flower, God's unfolding grace can gradually transform our difficult situations into something beautiful in His perfect timing. And even though it's harder some days to trust God, He really is working, and His ways are always best.

Just as God's grace fills our lives with goodness, you'll find plenty of goodness layered into every bite of 7-Layer Dip, each layer offering something delicious and satisfying: refried beans, sour cream, guacamole, cheddar cheese, and more! It's a delicious dip for a family gathering, a potluck, or game-watching. Enjoy digging into the layers of this dip, and as you do, let it be a reminder of the abundant grace God supplies you with each day: layer upon layer, grace upon grace, to help you in all your needs.

Lord, we are so grateful for Your abundant grace and how it transforms our weakness into strength when we put our faith in You. We thank You that, because of Your grace in our lives, we can live in victory no matter what comes our way. We know that we can release any burden we're carrying and give it over to You, no matter how big or small, and that Your grace will always be more than enough to get us through. There's just no end to Your grace; it overflows from You into our lives and redeems the hard, messy situations we face. It makes us strong in our weakest moments, bringing us hope and peace. We love You, Lord, and we praise You for being our faithful and loving Father, Protector, and Guide—and for all the ways Your grace continues to work in our lives. Amen.

7-layer dip

Dig into this dip that has layers upon layers of good things!

PREP: 25 MIN. | COOK: 0 MIN. | TOTAL TIME: 25 MIN. | SERVINGS: 10–12

1 (16-ounce) can refried beans

1⅓ cups sour cream, divided

1 (1.25-ounce) packet taco seasoning mix

2 cups guacamole

1½ cups shredded cheddar cheese

1 cup diced fresh tomatoes

⅓ cup chunky salsa

⅓ cup sliced green onions

¼ cup sliced black olives

Tortilla chips

1. In a medium-size bowl, mix the refried beans, ⅓ cup of the sour cream, and the taco seasoning mix, blending everything well.

2. On a large oval or round serving platter (or a deep-dish glass pie plate, if you want all the layers to show from the side), evenly spread the refried bean mixture. Next, spread the guacamole evenly over the refried bean layer, then spread the remaining 1 cup sour cream evenly over the guacamole layer.

3. Add the cheddar cheese next, sprinkling evenly over the sour cream layer. Then mix the diced tomatoes with the salsa and layer over the cheese.

4. Sprinkle the sliced green onions over the diced tomato/salsa layer, then add the last layer, a sprinkling of sliced black olives. Serve with tortilla chips.

spring cleaning

Put on your new nature, and be renewed as you learn to know your Creator and become like Him.
COLOSSIANS 3:10 NLT

One of the best things about springtime is the feeling of freshness it brings. As we open the windows of our homes, inviting the breezy spring air inside, we realize that it's that time of year—time to do our spring cleaning! Time to let go of dusty old things and embrace the clean and the new. Time to simplify and eliminate things we no longer need or want. Less clutter in our homes gives us more room to breathe, more peace.

As we clean and refresh our homes in this season, doesn't it make sense to do some spring cleaning in our hearts and minds too? Just as we bring a feeling of renewal to our homes as we let go of unwanted clutter, we can do the same for ourselves—letting go of things that keep us from growing deeper in our faith and our relationship with God. We need a deep cleaning inside of us!

How do we go about doing a spring cleaning in ourselves? Here are some ways:

Release things from the past. These could include worries, burdens we're carrying, past failures, or unpleasant memories. We can release these things from the past so we can move ahead into the fresh and new things God has for us.

Let go of negative thoughts. Maybe you tell yourself, *I can't do this*, or *I'm not good enough*. Recognize that these negative thoughts are lies, and focus on the truth of what God says about you—that you are His child (1 John 3:1), that you are wonderfully made (Psalm 139:14), and that He loves and delights in you (Zephaniah 3:17). Think positive, life-giving thoughts!

Discard unhelpful habits. Do you procrastinate? Do you spend too much time overthinking different scenarios in your head? Think about some habits you could do away with and ask God to help you eliminate them from your life.

Declutter your days. Are your days filled with so many things that it feels like it's hard to keep your head above water? Pray about what activities or commitments you could eliminate from your schedule so you have time to catch your breath and recharge a little. Don't neglect making time for yourself!

As you're spring cleaning your home, you may work up an appetite, so take a break and enjoy this Bacon-Ranch Cheese Ball. It's so easy to make, and perfect for snacking while you and your family or guests spend time together. The combination of savory flavors is so good! As you're enjoying this cheese ball, take the time to think about what things in your heart and mind you could toss out to make room for more of God's peace and joy. It will take a little work, as all spring cleaning does, but with His grace and strength, you can do it!

God, create a clean heart for me and renew a steadfast spirit within me.
PSALM 51:10 CSB

"Clean what is inside the cup first, and then the outside will be clean too!"
MATTHEW 23:26 GNT

You can't go back and change the beginning, but you can start where you are and change the ending.
C. S. LEWIS

He can be depended on to forgive us and to cleanse us from every wrong.
I JOHN 1:9 TLB

The Lord says, "Do not cling to events of the past or dwell on what happened long ago."
ISAIAH 43:18 GNT

Being a Christian is more than just an instantaneous conversion— it is a daily process whereby you grow to be more and more like Christ.
CHARLES SPURGEON

bacon-ranch cheese ball

Take a break and enjoy this easy-to-make snack! You'll need to refrigerate the cheese ball for two hours before you add the coating.

PREP: 20 MIN. | COOK: 0 MIN. | TOTAL TIME: 2 HRS. 20 MIN. | SERVINGS: 16

- 2 (8-ounce) packages cream cheese, softened
- 1 (1-ounce) package dry ranch dressing mix
- 2 tablespoons mayonnaise
- ½ teaspoon garlic powder
- ½ cup chopped green onions, divided
- ¾ cup real bacon pieces, divided
- 2 cups finely shredded cheddar cheese, divided
- ⅓ cup chopped pecans
- Crackers, for serving

1. In a large bowl, mix the cream cheese, ranch dressing mix, mayonnaise, and garlic powder. Then mix in half of the green onions, half of the bacon pieces, and 1½ cups of the cheddar cheese. Mix everything well.

2. Form mixture into a round ball (mixture will be sticky, so coat hands with cooking spray to shape the ball or use a piece of plastic wrap to cover your hands). Wrap in plastic wrap and refrigerate for at least 2 hours.

3. Make the mixture to coat the cheese ball: In small bowl, mix together the remaining green onions, bacon pieces, cheddar cheese, and chopped pecans. Spread this mixture evenly onto a large platter.

4. Remove plastic wrap from chilled cheese ball and roll in the mixture on the platter, completely covering the ball and lightly pressing the mixture into the ball so it sticks. (You'll have more than enough of the mixture to coat your cheese ball. You can add the extra to a salad if you'd like.)

5. Place cheese ball on a cheese board or serving plate and serve with crackers. If serving later, refrigerate cheese ball until ready to serve.

refreshed and renewed

*"I will satisfy those who are weary,
and I will refresh every soul."*
JEREMIAH 31:25 THE VOICE

What would it look like to get up early every morning to spend quiet time with your Creator? Your alarm goes off but you're not quite ready to get out of bed. But as you lie there not wanting to move, something nudges you inside and you remember how soothing it is to spend one-on-one time with your Savior. So you get up, make your coffee, and settle in your comfy chair. And as you sit there, you pour out your heart to God. You give Him all your worries and concerns about the day ahead; you thank Him for all the goodness He has in store for your life; you ask Him to be involved in every decision and every detail of what is to come. And your soul sits in His presence, refreshed and ready. Before you ever walk out the door, you are filled with indescribable peace and unshakable strength.

Quiet time with God is so renewing to our souls. In today's world, it's so easy to get caught up in our busy schedules, running from work to home to church to school to extracurricular activities to our second jobs, and before we know it, we've missed out on our quiet time with God. We've missed out on the only time that doesn't take from us, but gives us refreshment and renewal.

God loves us so much, He wants to spend time with us and speak to our hearts—every single day! So how do we find the time to do that? Maybe try starting with five or ten minutes each morning, praying and reading Scriptures. Then, if possible, gradually increase your time. You can also use pockets of time during your day—like when you're waiting in line to pick up the kids from school—to pray. Or when you're in the waiting room for an appointment, use that time to pray and read Scripture. Preparing a meal? Refresh your mind with prayer as you spend time in the kitchen. (If you need an idea for a side dish, try the recipe for Refreshing Fruit Salad. You can pray or sing a worship song as you cut up the fruit and toss it all together.) Ask God to show you other ways you can use moments in your day to spend time with Him. Our times of quiet with the Lord can be day-changing and life-changing. Let's draw close to Him, ready to hear what He wants to say to us and ready to be refreshed and renewed by His presence!

Lord, You're always there for us, whether it's in the quiet of the morning or in the middle of a chaotic day. Thank You for speaking to us each day through Your Word and Your still, small voice, telling us exactly what we need to hear. You take such good care of us throughout our day, going before us, keeping us safe, and making our way smooth. You replace our anxious thoughts with Your peace and our weariness with Your strength. You are always so faithful to take care of our every need. Thank You for the refreshing and renewing work You do in our hearts, minds, and souls when we focus on You and spend time with You. You fill our lives with so much goodness, Lord, and we are so grateful. We love You so much. Amen.

refreshing fruit salad

This recipe makes a large salad, perfect for potlucks or larger family gatherings. To make a smaller salad, just divide the ingredients in half.

PREP: 50 MIN. | COOK: 0 MIN. | TOTAL TIME: 50 MIN. | SERVINGS: 10–12

- 6 cups bite-size chunks cantaloupe (about 1 melon)
- 6 cups bite-size chunks honeydew (about 1 melon)
- 3 cups red or green seedless grapes
- 2½ cups strawberries, hulled and halved or quartered (about 16 ounces)
- 1 (15-ounce) can mandarin oranges, rinsed and drained
- 1 (20-ounce) can pineapple chunks in 100% juice, drained, but save the juice!

1. In a large bowl, add the cantaloupe and honeydew chunks, grapes, strawberries, mandarin oranges, and pineapple chunks. Toss fruit together to evenly distribute.

2. Drizzle the remaining pineapple juice from the can over the fruit salad and toss again. Serve immediately or refrigerate until ready to serve (toss fruit salad again just before serving).

a well-watered garden

"I will always guide you and satisfy you with good things. I will keep you strong and well. You will be like a garden that has plenty of water, like a spring of water that never goes dry."

ISAIAH 58:11 GNT

Every spring, gardeners prepare the soil to plant flower and vegetable seeds. As the seeds sprout, the gardeners care for the seedlings, watering and weeding each one, so they can thrive.

Just as gardeners care for their flower and vegetable gardens, God, the Master Gardener, cares for His entire creation. Psalm 104:13 (NLT) says: "You send rain on the mountains from Your heavenly home, and You fill the earth with the fruit of Your labor." Because of Him, the mountain streams flow, the grass grows, the trees provide shade for the animals. God provides for each one of us too. Though He doesn't always do things the way we wish, He watches over every need we have.

Because of God's great love and care for us, we don't need to worry about anything. In I Peter 5:7 (TLB) we're reminded, "Let Him have all your worries and cares, for He is always thinking about you and watching everything that concerns you." Worry, anxiety, and fear are like weeds growing in our minds and hearts—they can overtake the good things, like peace, joy, and hope, that God plants in us. How do we get rid of these weeds? As we come to God daily in prayer and give our worries to Him, He pulls out our "weeds" of worry. Whenever anything that causes us to be anxious comes our way, we can give it to God. What does it mean to give it to God? Well, it means memorizing Scriptures such as Philippians 4:6 and repeating it every time fear creeps in your thoughts. It means having an honest conversation about your true feelings and your deepest secrets with your Father. It means getting to a place where you can completely surrender not only your worries, but your life to Him. His hands are open to receive all of us. And as we release these weeds of worry and fear, there's more room for God to plant His peace, strength, and joy in our hearts. And He never stops working in us; He continues to water us and refresh us, so we never run dry. He gives us the strength we need to keep going and growing.

Gardening is especially rewarding when you get to see the flowers bloom and the vegetables ripen, knowing that your care and patience have helped them grow. For this next recipe, why not seek out fresh-from-the-garden veggies? If you don't have a garden, you can find these at your nearest farmers market. And as you're preparing and arranging the salad ingredients, thank God for His provision as you enjoy the bounty. And thank Him for His love, care, and all the ways He is working in you, bringing beautiful growth to the garden of your heart.

It was God . . . who made the garden grow in your hearts. . . .
God is important because He is the one
who makes things grow.
I CORINTHIANS 3:6–7 TLB

Do not be anxious about anything, but in every situation,
by prayer and petition, with thanksgiving,
present your requests to God.
PHILIPPIANS 4:6 NIV

Faith grows when it is planted
in the fertile soil of God's Word.
BILLY GRAHAM

Let our gardener, God, landscape you with the
Word, making a salvation-garden of your life.
JAMES 1:21 THE MESSAGE

You have been reborn—not from seed
that eventually dies but from seed that is eternal—
through the word of God that lives and endures forever.
I PETER 1:23 THE VOICE

Live . . . a life Jesus will be proud of: bountiful in fruits
from the soul, making Jesus Christ attractive to all, getting
everyone involved in the glory and praise of God.
PHILIPPIANS 1:11 THE MESSAGE

easy cobb salad

Make this salad as a side dish, or have it for a meal!

PREP: 45 MIN. | COOK: 0 MIN. | TOTAL TIME: 45 MIN. | SERVINGS: 4–6

7 to 8 cups romaine lettuce or mixed greens, chopped

12 slices bacon, cooked and crumbled (about ¾ cup)

3 hard-boiled eggs, chopped

2½ cups cooked chicken, chopped

1 cup cherry tomatoes, halved

1 avocado, peeled, pitted, and diced

½ cup crumbled blue cheese

½ cup red onion, diced

Your favorite dressing

1. In a large salad bowl, arrange the chopped romaine lettuce or mixed salad greens in an even layer.

2. Top greens with the crumbled bacon, hard-boiled eggs, chopped chicken, cherry tomatoes, diced avocado, crumbled blue cheese, and diced red onion, arranging these ingredients in rows.

3. Serve in small salad bowls with your favorite salad dressing, such as ranch or Italian, or vinaigrette, such as balsamic.

NOTE: To save time in making the salad, cook the bacon and chicken ahead of time, or use leftover or rotisserie chicken and pre-cooked-and-crumbled real bacon.

incomparable

**Thank You for making me so wonderfully complex!
Your workmanship is marvelous—
how well I know it.**

PSALM 139:14 NLT

Here's something you might need to hear today: You are *incomparable*! There's no one else exactly like you and there never will be—you are a true original. God lovingly created every detail about you. Psalm 139:13 (NLT) says: "You made all the delicate, inner parts of my body and knit me together in my mother's womb." God did that for every single one of us. With the greatest of care, He created the delicate, complex parts of our beings. He crafted and designed us, or *knit* us together. To knit something is to create something handmade—beautiful, unique, and treasured. We all know that making something handmade takes time, skill, and patience. And handmade items are also made with so much love. That's why they are such treasures to us. In the same way, we have all been lovingly and skillfully created by God, and we are so precious to Him.

Since each one of us is a treasure in God's eyes, why do we compare ourselves with others? We might think we're not as talented as someone else or as organized or productive . . . and that can fill us with insecurity and discouragement. We might feel like we just don't measure up—that we're not good enough. But we are more than good enough! We are God's handiwork, and He created us with just the right giftings and abilities to fulfill the special purpose He has for us. In Galatians 6:4 (NLT) we're told, "Pay careful attention to your own work, for then you will get the satisfaction of a job well done, and you won't need to compare yourself to anyone else." God doesn't want us to waste time comparing ourselves to others. Let's embrace the uniquely wonderful way God made us instead!

We can do this by thanking God for making us so "wonderfully complex." He crafted us perfectly and designed us skillfully to fulfill our calling. Each of us is created to be different from everyone else. We're one of a kind, and our differences can be unique ways we can glorify and shine for Him. When we look at things in this way, we can be grateful about how God designed us and be excited about how He uses us and will use us in the future.

When it comes to making dinner, this Chicken-Broccoli Rice Casserole is pretty incomparable too! Chicken, broccoli, and rice are blended in a creamy, cheesy soup mixture, and it's all topped with buttery cracker crumbs. As you mix all the ingredients together and sprinkle on the crumb topping, remember that you were created to be like no one else in this world—and thank the Lord for how wonderfully incomparable He made you!

Lord, it's amazing how You have made each one of us so wonderfully complex and unique, and that You know each one of us by name. You know us so personally and completely—better than we know ourselves! Thank You for creating us with such care. We are each handmade and knit together so skillfully by You. It brings us joy to know that we are precious and treasured in Your eyes. Help us to remember that, because we are beautifully created by You, there is no need to compare anything about ourselves to others. Instead, remind us to embrace our own uniqueness and be grateful for the gifts and talents You've given us. Let us never forget that each one of us is incomparable. And fill us with appreciation for the way You've uniquely created others, so we can celebrate and encourage them. Amen.

chicken broccoli rice casserole

*This casserole has a great buttery cracker topping.
Or save some time and just sprinkle the top with some French-fried onions!*

PREP: 20 MIN. | COOK: 35 MIN. | TOTAL TIME: 55 MIN. | SERVINGS: 9–12

- 2 (10.5-ounce) cans condensed cream of chicken soup
- ⅓ cup chicken broth
- ½ cup sour cream
- ⅔ cup mayonnaise
- Dash of salt, pepper, and garlic powder
- 1 (12-ounce) bag frozen broccoli florets, thawed
- 2 cups chicken, cooked and diced or shredded
- 2 cups cooked rice
- 3 cups shredded cheddar cheese, divided
- 2 cups crushed buttery round crackers (about 42)
- ⅓ cup butter, melted

1. Preheat oven to 350°F. Grease or spray a 9 x 13-inch pan or baking dish with nonstick spray; set aside.

2. In a large mixing bowl, stir together the condensed soup (undiluted), chicken broth, sour cream, mayonnaise, salt, pepper, garlic powder, thawed broccoli, chicken, rice, and 2 cups of the shredded cheese (save the remaining 1 cup for sprinkling on top).

3. Spread mixture evenly in prepared 9 × 13-inch pan or baking dish. Sprinkle with the remaining 1 cup shredded cheddar cheese.

4. Mix the crushed crackers with the melted butter in a small bowl until crumbs are moistened, then sprinkle evenly over the top of the casserole.

5. Bake at 350°F, uncovered, for 30 to 35 minutes, until bubbly at edges and broccoli is tender. Let cool for about 5 minutes, then serve.

breathe in god's goodness

**He Himself gives life and breath to everything,
and He satisfies every need.**

ACTS 17:25 NLT

When you have a hard day, do you ever pause and take a long, deep breath? There's something calming about clearing your mind and breathing in deep. Going for a walk is even better—it's a great way to soothe your anxious thoughts and be reminded that even on busy or difficult days, God is in control. When you're out in nature on a beautiful day, it's impossible *not* to notice all the goodness around you! Through God's creation, we can see His glory in the simplest of ways. The radiance of the sun reminds us of His everlasting light. The air we breathe reminds us that He is our source of life, our breath of life. The gentle rain reminds us of His tender care. Nature reveals to us how gracious, caring, powerful, and loving God is and helps us turn our focus on Him instead of our worries.

No time to go for a walk? You can still pause, breathe in, and focus on God wherever you're at or whatever you're doing. Driving to work during rush hour? Breathe in and remember this: "You can be sure that God will take care of everything you need" (Philippians 4:19 The Message). Winding down after a long day? Breathe in and embrace the truth that God is always in control: "Do not be afraid or discouraged, for the Lord will personally go ahead of you. He will be with you" (Deuteronomy 31:8 NLT).

During the beauty of the spring season, as we celebrate Easter, we also remember and reflect on the resurrection of Jesus and the new life we have in Him: "Anyone who belongs to Christ has become a new person. The old life is gone; a new life has begun!" (II Corinthians 5:17 NLT). That helps put everything into perspective. He gives new life to everything, and in Him we have all we need. Because of this promise, and because we can see God in nature and hear Him speak through His Word, we can live our days full of hope and joy—no matter how busy or challenging life gets.

Wherever we are, whether we're outside in His creation or inside making Easter treats, like these Easter Egg Blondies, we can breathe in and focus on God's goodness. The candy-coated chocolate eggs that are sprinkled on top of these blondies are sweet reminders of His love and care for us, just as He cares for the birds nesting in the trees. He, who gives life and breath to everything, will take care of every need you have.

*Ever since the world was created,
people have seen the earth and sky.
Through everything God made,
they can clearly see His invisible qualities—
His eternal power and divine nature.*
ROMANS 1:20 NLT

*The heavens proclaim the glory of God.
The skies display His craftsmanship.*
PSALM 19:1 NLT

*"If God cares so wonderfully for wildflowers
. . . He will certainly care for you."*
MATTHEW 6:30 NLT

*Thou hast made us for Thyself and restless is
our heart until it comes to rest in Thee.*
SAINT AUGUSTINE

*The life of every living thing is in His hand, and
the breath of every human being.*
JOB 12:10 NLT

*The Lord is good to everyone. He showers
compassion on all His creation.*
PSALM 145:9 NLT

Let the peace that comes from Christ rule in your hearts.
COLOSSIANS 3:15 NLT

easter egg blondies

Make these for Easter or anytime in the spring!

PREP: 15 MIN. | COOK: 30 MIN. | TOTAL TIME: 45 MIN. | SERVINGS: 9–12

½ cup (1 stick) butter, melted (you can use salted or unsalted)

¾ cup light brown sugar, packed

1 large egg

1½ teaspoons pure vanilla extract

1 cup all-purpose flour

½ teaspoon baking powder

½ teaspoon salt

1 (10-ounce) package Cadbury Mini Eggs, divided (chop 1 cup of the mini eggs to stir into the batter and keep the rest, almost ½ cup, whole to scatter on top)

1. Preheat oven to 350°F. Grease an 8 x 8-inch square baking pan or line with parchment paper; set aside.

2. In a large or medium-size bowl, add the melted butter and brown sugar, blending well. Then add the egg and vanilla extract, mixing everything well. Next, add the flour, baking powder, and salt, mixing until all ingredients are combined (do not over-mix).

3. Fold in the 1 cup chopped mini eggs and mix until evenly distributed in batter. Pour batter into prepared baking pan, spreading it evenly.

4. Bake for 20 minutes, then remove from oven briefly to scatter and slightly press the remaining mini eggs on top; bake for an additional 10 minutes, until edges are golden and center is set (a toothpick inserted in the center should come out clean).

5. Cool completely in pan, then cut into squares.

NOTE: An easy way to "chop" the mini eggs is to put them in a zip top bag and crush into chunky pieces with a rolling pin.

filled up

**I pray that God, the source of hope,
will fill you completely with joy
and peace because you trust in Him.
Then you will overflow with confident hope
through the power of the Holy Spirit.**
ROMANS 15:13 NLT

What does having a "full life" mean? For some, it might mean a life filled with good things—a loving family, a nice house, good friends. For others, it could mean a "busy life" filled with lots of activities and responsibilities—taking care of kids, working on home projects, having a dream job. These are things we enjoy, and when all is going well, life feels full and good. But when things aren't going that well—the kids are sick, the home project didn't turn out the way we thought it would, we're having to work extra hours—life doesn't seem so great. There are times when our schedule is packed with so much to do, we can't fit one more thing into our day. We're tired, worn out, and feeling "empty." We need to be "filled up" and restored.

We can fill our physical bodies with food to give us energy and we can rest when we're tired, but how do we get "filled up" spiritually in our hearts, minds, and souls? That's where true restoration happens—and it's something only God can do. As we spend time in the Word and in prayer each day, we can ask Him to fill us with the power and strength of His Spirit. And to continue to fill us every day. Nothing and no one can strengthen us like God can. That's what being "filled up" and having a full life is all about.

This "filling up" helps equip us to deal with whatever comes our way each day. God loves to pour His power and strength into us, and that's how our spirits are restored. He replaces our emptiness with fruitfulness. "The Holy Spirit produces this kind of fruit in our lives: love, joy, peace, patience, kindness, goodness, faithfulness, gentleness, and self-control" (Galatians 5:22–23 NLT). The more the fruit of the Spirit grows and flourishes in our lives, the more we reflect God's character and love to others. And the better equipped we are to do whatever He is calling us to do.

What a blessing to have this gift of a "filled up" life! And speaking of being "filled up," these Lemon-Filled Cupcakes have a lemon curd filling that gives them a wonderful springtime taste. They're a delicious way to remember that God fills us with exactly what we need and that He fills our lives "with good things" (Psalm 103:5 NLT)!

Lord, we thank You that You are a God of restoration. We know that only You can renew and refill our minds, hearts, and souls when we're feeling empty, like we have nothing left to give. Only You can give us what we need to live our lives to the fullest. We ask that You fill us to overflowing every day with the strength and power of Your Holy Spirit and with confident hope in Your promises. As You help us grow stronger, let our lives become more and more fruitful, overflowing with love, joy, peace, patience, kindness, goodness, faithfulness, gentleness, and self-control. Help us to grow in the fruit of the Spirit so we can be reflections of Your love and grace to others. We thank You, Father, for blessing us abundantly—for always pouring so much goodness into our lives. You are a generous Father, and because of Your love and care, we never lack for anything. Amen.

lemon-filled cupcakes

*These cupcakes are filled with a lemon curd filling.
Use your favorite brand.*

PREP: 30 MIN. | COOK: 12–17 MIN. | TOTAL TIME: 1 HR. | SERVINGS: 24

- 1 (15.25-ounce) box lemon cake mix
- Ingredients to prepare cake mix (water, oil, eggs)
- 1 (11-ounce) jar lemon curd (or strawberry or blueberry jam)
- 1 (16-ounce) container lemon frosting
- Optional: Zest of 1 large lemon and/or white coarse decorating sugar, for sprinkling on top
- Supplies: Apple corer or small paring knife to make cupcake holes; a small spoon for filling the cupcakes

1. Line two 12-cup muffin tins with paper liners; set aside.
2. Make cupcakes according to directions on cake mix box, also following instructions for baking. After cupcakes are baked, let them cool completely.
3. Cut a round hole in the center of each cupcake, about the size of a penny, going about halfway down into the cupcake. You can use an apple corer or small paring knife to do this. (I think an apple corer works the best.)
4. Using a small spoon, fill each cupcake hole with lemon curd, or strawberry or blueberry jam.
5. Frost the cupcakes with the lemon frosting: First, place a small dollop of frosting in the center of each cupcake to cover the filling, then add as much additional frosting as desired and spread over the entire top of each cupcake.
6. Top frosted cupcakes with a sprinkling of lemon zest or white coarse decorating sugar—or a little of both! Keep refrigerated until ready to serve.

sweet and simple

**"Accept God's kingdom
in the simplicity of a child."**
LUKE 18:17 THE MESSAGE

Did you grow up in a home where you always had food to eat, clothes to wear, toys to play with, and a comfortable bed to sleep in? Maybe you had parents who made sure you had everything you needed in life—parents you could turn to when something unexpected came up—parents you could count on to help.

For many of us, it wasn't until we entered adulthood that we realized just how much our parents were doing for us. Not only did they provide all the meals, clothes, and comforts of home, they loved us even in our disobedience and took care of us when we were sick. Because they watched over us, we didn't have to worry about our needs. When you think about it, the care of a loving parent mirrors the care our heavenly Father gives us: unconditional love, provision, protection, comfort, guidance, patience, and forgiveness. It's so comforting to know that God loves and cares for each one of us that way!

God wants us to come to Him with all of our needs because we are His children and He is always there for us—always watching over us. Psalm 121:3 (NIV) says, "He will not let your foot slip—He who watches over you will not slumber." He doesn't want us to be weighed down with burdens. He wants to take those on for us as we come to Him with the simple, trusting faith of a child—running to His open arms, letting His love and presence surround us. Jesus tells us in Matthew 6:26 (THE VOICE), "Look at the birds in the sky. . . . They do not sow or reap—and yet, they are always fed because your heavenly Father feeds them. And you are even more precious to Him than a beautiful bird. If He looks after them, of course He will look after you." The word *precious* means "of great value" and "highly esteemed." That's how God sees us. He loves us and values us so much and wants the very best for us.

When you were a child, did you spend time in the kitchen with your parents or grandparents making cookies? It's sweet, simple moments like this we remember, sharing time with the people we love. God also yearns for us to draw near to Him and spend sweet moments in His presence. Let the next time you make cookies be a reminder of that! If you want to make some quick and easy cookies, Strawberry Crinkle Cookies are so simple and good—and you can let the kids help! Or if you're making them yourself, you can spend time talking to Jesus about your day as you're stirring up the dough. He holds you close, loves you, and cares for you more than you can know!

*The Lord is like a father to His children,
tender and compassionate to those who fear Him.*
PSALM 103:13 NLT

*"Whoever becomes simple
and elemental again,
like this child, will rank high
in God's kingdom."*
MATTHEW 18:4 THE MESSAGE

*Give all your worries and cares to God,
for He cares about you.*
1 PETER 5:7 NLT

*Each day of our lives we make deposits in
the memory banks of our children.*
CHUCK SWINDOLL

*"I will teach you and tell you the way to go
and how to get there; I will give you good
counsel, and I will watch over you."*
PSALM 32:8 THE VOICE

*In Christ Jesus you are all children
of God through faith.*
GALATIANS 3:26 NIV

strawberry crinkle cookies

Sweet and colorful cookies for spring!

PREP: 15 MIN. | COOK: 10–11 MIN. | TOTAL TIME: 26 MIN. | SERVINGS: 18–20

1 (15.25-ounce) box strawberry cake mix

2 large eggs

⅓ cup canola oil or vegetable oil

½ cup powdered sugar, to roll the cookie dough in

1. Preheat oven to 350°F. Line two cookie sheets with parchment paper; set aside.

2. Put powdered sugar in a small bowl and set aside.

3. In a medium-size bowl, combine the dry cake mix, eggs, and oil, mixing until ingredients are combined well and a soft dough forms.

4. Using your hands, a spoon, or a cookie scoop, form cookie dough into 1½-inch balls and roll balls in powdered sugar to completely coat. Place on prepared cookie sheets about 2 inches apart.

5. Bake for 10 to 11 minutes, until the tops of the cookies are crackly and centers of cookies are set. Remove from oven, and after 1 to 2 minutes, transfer cookies from cookie sheets to wire racks and cool completely.

THE CHANGING SEASONS:
spring-summer

As the breezy days of spring turn into the relaxing days of summer, we can look back and be thankful for all the ways we experienced God's goodness in the months that have passed by. Spring brought us the anticipation of new beginnings and the wonder of watching new life begin to grow all around us. It also reminded us of the new life we have because of Jesus and how our souls are nourished and refreshed spending time with Him. We did some spring cleaning in our homes and our hearts, discarding unnecessary clutter to make room for the important things, and we learned that sweet and helpful words are like honey—life-giving to others. We discovered the comfort of releasing our cares and burdens to God—things we weren't ever meant to carry—and the importance of embracing the beautiful, unique, one-of-a-kind way God created each of us. And we are encouraged by this truth: that in the busy days of this season and every season, when we don't know how we'll get it all done, God never fails to give us the grace, strength, and help we need.

As much as we love springtime, we still look forward to all that summer brings. It's a season when we live a little more simply and enjoy more time outdoors. We linger over morning coffee on the patio and enjoy simple meals in the backyard—like grilled burgers, potato salad, and thick slices of watermelon. We go to the kids' softball games, try to squeeze in time for evening walks, and admire the incredible sunsets as the longer days fade into evening. Somehow, life seems to slow down a little in the summer.

Even though it's a simpler, slower season for many of us, summer is also a time of growth. We see this while we're out enjoying nature—gardens flourishing and trees getting taller and branching out wider. Psalm 147:8 (NIV) says, "He covers the sky with clouds; He supplies the earth with rain and makes grass grow on the hills." Everything is vibrant and thriving. In a similar way, God continues to work in us and bring growth to our spiritual lives. He wants us to flourish. He can renew our minds as we grow. The growth will show in the words we speak and the way we live our lives. "Don't copy the behavior and customs of this world, but let God transform you into a new person by changing the way you think" (Romans 12:2 NLT). Because of this transforming work God can do in us, we have so much to look forward to. His plans for us are "good and pleasing and perfect" (Romans 12:2 NLT). Let this summer be a season when we continue to grow closer to God, bloom lavishly, and embrace all that He has for us!

Lord, we thank You for the beauty of spring and for all the ways we've seen Your goodness this season. We're so grateful as we reflect on the new life we have because of Jesus and all the other fresh, new beginnings You give us. You delight in doing new things in our lives, our hearts, our minds, our souls, and in everything all around us. You're in all the details of our days and seasons, watching over us and guiding us, and we're thankful to You for loving us so well. As we move into summer, we ask that You surround us with Your peace as we take breaks to relax and enjoy Your creation. Protect us and keep our families safe as we travel. And let this be a season of abundant growth for us, Father, as You continue to do a transforming work in us—helping us grow closer to You and stronger in our faith. We thank You and give You glory for all You are and all You do. Amen.

summer

*Walk into the fields and look at the wildflowers.
They don't fuss with their appearance—
but have you ever seen color and design quite like it?*

LUKE 12:27 THE MESSAGE

As we see wildflowers blooming, vegetables sprouting, and fruit getting ripe for picking, we're reminded not only of God's creativity and artistry, but also of the abundance He fills our lives with. From the farms and fields and the groves and gardens, He blesses us with all the refreshing tastes of summer. We love those slices of sweet honeydew melon for breakfast, cherries picked from the tree for eating fresh, and the zesty taste of a tall glass of lemonade! Then there's corn on the cob, drenched with melted butter, and baskets of crisp cucumbers, vine-ripe tomatoes, and colorful bell peppers to enjoy all summer long. God's abundance is so amazing!

Summer is a season of abounding growth in nature—and God wants that for our lives too. As we spend time with Him every day—reading His Word, praying, and taking time to "be still" and listen to Him—we grow spiritually. Paul describes this kind of growth in Philippians 1:9-11 (GNT), "I pray that your love will keep on growing more and more, together with true knowledge and perfect judgment, so that you will be able to choose what is best. . . . Your lives will be filled with the truly good qualities which only Jesus Christ can produce."

As we enter into summer, let's remember not to miss the beauty thriving all around us. Why not get up early and watch the sunrise, spend a family weekend at the lake, go for a bike ride at the park, and enjoy the longer, brighter days? And let's continue to thrive as we grow closer to God, abounding in love and an ever-stronger faith.

a new day and new mercies

The faithful love of the Lord never ends! His mercies never cease. Great is His faithfulness; His mercies begin afresh each morning.
LAMENTATIONS 3:22–23 NLT

As the sun peeks out over the horizon and a new day dawns, it's a glorious reminder that God's mercies are new every morning. The challenges and difficulties of yesterday are behind us, and God can give us a fresh start today. He can replace any discouragement we have with hope, and He is faithful to provide what we need to get through this day. We can find comfort and strength in knowing that His mercies "never cease"; His love, compassion, and care are abundant and unlimited.

Still, it's easy to fall into an anxious mindset. Sometimes we start stressing about the day ahead as soon as it begins, with so many different details to take care of at home and work. But God's Word reminds us that joy comes in the morning: "The deepest pains may linger through the night, but joy greets the soul with the smile of morning" (Psalm 30:5 THE VOICE). Just as the light of morning replaces the darkness of night, the darkness of our worries is overcome by the light of God's love and mercy. Each sunrise is a reminder of that. God is always faithful to lead us step by step throughout our day, guiding us and filling us with His strength and peace. Even when we don't understand or can't see how God is working in our day, we can be confident knowing He is in control and taking care of us.

Sometimes we struggle with the fear that we've "messed up"—that we've made mistakes or bad choices and have ruined the good plans God has for us. Nothing could be further from the truth! Our merciful God can redeem any mistakes we make or hard situations we are going through. He is the God of new beginnings and second, third, and unlimited chances. He loves to bless us with fresh starts and turn the messy parts of our lives into something beautiful.

The next time you are connecting with your compassionate, loving, faithful Father, why not thank Him for all the goodness and mercy He fills your life with? After all, He gives us so much to be grateful for!

As you mix and pour the ingredients in today's recipe, Blueberry Chip Muffins, try to keep a heart of gratitude. Muffins make an easy, convenient breakfast, and summer is the perfect season to enjoy this recipe, since they're made with fresh blueberries! You can make them the night before so they'll be ready for you in the morning. And you can do what Psalm 92:2 (TLB) says: "Every morning tell Him, 'Thank You for Your kindness,' and every evening rejoice in all His faithfulness."

> *Satisfy us in the morning with Your unfailing love,*
> *that we may sing for joy and be glad all our days.*
> **PSALM 90:14 NIV**

> *Oh, how sweet the light of day, and how wonderful*
> *to live in the sunshine! . . . Don't take a single day for*
> *granted. Take delight in each light-filled hour.*
> **ECCLESIASTES 11:7-8 THE MESSAGE**

> *Oh, that we might know the Lord!*
> *Let us press on to know Him. He will respond*
> *to us as surely as the arrival of dawn.*
> **HOSEA 6:3 NLT**

> *Each morning is a new beginning of our life.*
> **DIETRICH BONHOEFFER**

> *Make up a song like none other.*
> *Sing a new song to the Eternal.*
> *And let His praise echo clear across the earth.*
> **ISAIAH 42:10 THE VOICE**

> *Let your face smile on us, Lord. . . .*
> *In peace I will lie down and sleep,*
> *for You alone, O Lord, will keep me safe.*
> **PSALM 4:6, 8 NLT**

blueberry chip muffins

You can substitute milk chocolate or semisweet chocolate chips for the white chocolate chips.

PREP: 15 MIN. | COOK: 23–25 MIN. | TOTAL TIME: 40 MIN. | SERVINGS: 12

- 1⅔ cups all-purpose flour
- ¾ cup granulated sugar
- ½ teaspoon salt
- 1 tablespoon baking powder
- ⅓ cup canola oil or light olive oil
- 1 large egg
- 1 teaspoon vanilla extract
- ⅓ cup plus 1 tablespoon half-and-half (light cream)
- 1 cup fresh blueberries
- ¾ cup white chocolate chips

1. Preheat oven to 350°F. Line a muffin pan with 12 paper liners; set aside.
2. In a medium-size bowl, blend flour, sugar, salt, and baking powder.
3. In a small bowl, mix the oil, egg, and vanilla extract, then mix in the half-and-half. Pour into the flour mixture and mix everything together until just combined.
4. Fold in the blueberries and white chocolate chips.
5. Spoon batter into the prepared muffin cups. Bake for 23 to 25 minutes, until a toothpick inserted in the center comes out clean.

growing strong roots

**Christ will make His home
in your hearts as you trust in Him.
Your roots will grow down
into God's love and keep you strong.**

EPHESIANS 3:17 NLT

Step outside on a summer day, and you can't miss the colorful abundance of the season! All the flowers, plants, trees, and bushes are so alive and vibrant. The seeds planted in the spring that took root and sprouted are now growing taller and sprawling wider. The roots of all these thriving plants and trees are growing deeper, and branches are filled with lush green leaves and ripening fruit. God's creation shows us how beautiful and fruitful this kind of strong and stable growth can be when roots run strong and deep.

For trees, plants, and bushes to develop strong roots, they need nourishment from the soil, sunlight, and water. These basic elements help plants and trees get anchored securely so they can stand up to heavy winds and storms. Their roots give them strength and stability below the ground as well as beautiful growth above the soil. Just as plants and trees need to be strongly rooted to grow well, we need to develop strong spiritual roots to grow and thrive. Having deep, strong roots keeps us steady and stable when the storms of life and windy days come our way. We can stay strong and secure in God's love through any difficulties or challenges we face when our faith is rooted deeply in Him and we know He is in control and taking care of us. And because of that, even in the hard times, we can still flourish in our hearts and minds with peace, confidence, and hope.

How do we grow strong roots? We develop them when we get our strength and nourishment from God and His Word. That's the "rich soil" we need to grow in. Colossians 2:7 (TLB) says, "Let your roots grow down into Him and draw up nourishment from Him. See that you go on growing in the Lord, and become strong and vigorous in the truth." The light that we need daily for wisdom and guidance is found in His Word too: "The unfolding of Your words gives light; it gives understanding" (Psalm 119:130 NIV). His Word also "waters" us, refreshing and sustaining us: "Let anyone who is thirsty come to Me and drink" (John 7:37 NIV). Rich soil, light, and water . . . through God's Word, we receive all the nourishment we need to stay strong.

Think of the beautiful blossoms and fruit of a cherry tree. We see beautiful growth above the ground while the roots of the tree grow strong below the ground, keeping it steady. Even in a summer storm, the beauty of the leafy, fruit-bearing branches is still evident above the soil. It's a comfort to know that whatever comes our way, when we're rooted and grounded in God and His Word, we have the strength we need, and we can continue to grow in beautiful ways. Making a Cherry-Almond Coffee Cake might help you remember that! As you enjoy it for breakfast or later in the day with coffee or tea, reflect on the ways God has provided the strength you've needed on busy days or in hard seasons, and thank Him for the anchor of His secure and loving care.

Lord, we're amazed at the beauty we see all around us in Your creation—all the intricate details—and that You spoke it all into being! The earth is so full of life and filled with Your goodness. We are humbled because, with all the millions of things going on in this world, You are always there for us. There is never a time when You are too busy for us to come to You. Your arms are always open, and You're always ready to surround us with Your peace and fill us with Your strength. You know our needs, cares, and worries, and You take time to speak to us through Your Word and in the quiet of the day. We thank You that even in the difficult times, we can flourish and grow because we are rooted and grounded in You and the promises You give us in Your Word. You always hold us close and love us like no one else can, with the purest of love. Thank You, Father, for everything You are to us and for all that You do. Amen.

cherry-almond coffee cake

This coffee cake is made with cherry pie filling so you can enjoy it in any season!

PREP: 15 MIN. | COOK: 24 MIN. | TOTAL TIME: 39 MIN. | SERVINGS: 12

4 cups all-purpose baking mix

½ cup granulated sugar

¼ cup butter, melted

½ cup milk or almond milk

1½ teaspoons almond extract

3 large eggs

1 (21-ounce) can cherry pie filling

ALMOND GLAZE:

1 cup powdered sugar

1½ to 2 tablespoons milk, almond milk, or half-and-half (light cream)

¼ teaspoon almond extract

2 tablespoons sliced or chopped almonds, toasted or untoasted, for sprinkling on top

1. Preheat oven to 350°F. Grease bottom and sides of a 9 x 13-inch pan with butter or cooking spray.

2. In a large bowl, mix the baking mix, sugar, melted butter, milk, and almond extract. Then add the eggs and mix everything well. You'll end up with a very thick batter.

3. Spread two-thirds of the batter (about 2½ cups) into the bottom of the greased 9 x 13-inch pan. Spoon the pie filling over the batter and spread to about ¼ inch from the edges of the pan.

4. Drop the remaining batter in tablespoon-size dollops on top of the pie filling, spacing the dollops of batter evenly, 5 rows down and 3 across, for a total of 15 dollops.

5. Bake for 23 to 24 minutes, until top batter and edges of coffee cake just start to turn lightly brown. Don't overbake, or coffee cake will be too dry.

6. While the coffee cake is baking, make the almond glaze: Stir powdered sugar, milk (or half-and-half), and almond extract until smooth and creamy. If glaze is too thick to drizzle, add a little more milk.

7. Drizzle glaze over the coffee cake while still warm, then sprinkle with sliced or chopped almonds. Best served warm.

cultivating contentment

**I have learned to be content whatever the circumstances.
I know what it is to be in need, and I know what it is to have plenty. . . .
I can do all this through Him who gives me strength.**

PHILIPPIANS 4:11–13 NIV

What are some of the things that bring you contentment during the summer? Maybe it's reading a good book while you're relaxing on a hammock, collecting seashells on a sandy beach, or having friends over for a cookout. It's easy to be content while we're enjoying fun and relaxing times like these. But what if we're in the middle of a busy or hard season? How do we find contentment in the difficult times?

When Paul wrote his letter to the Philippians, he was in prison, experiencing a hard season. Yet despite his difficulties, he wrote to the believers in Philippi to express his gratitude for them and to encourage them. He also wanted them to know he was staying strong in his faith. He wrote that he had "learned the secret of being content in any and every situation"—in the good times and the hard times, in times of need and times of abundance.

How was this possible? The "secret," Paul shared, was his faith in Jesus. He knew Jesus could provide all he needed to get through any circumstance he faced: "I can do all this through Him who gives me strength." Contentment during times of struggle is cultivated when we rely on the Lord's strength and not our own. When we give our worries and burdens to Him, we can rest in the peace of knowing He is taking care of us and supplying us with the strength we need. But how do we simply hand our burdens over to Him? It's easier said than done. And sometimes it means you surrender the same worry over to Him time and time again. But the more you pray and recite Scripture and start to acknowledge your limitations, the more you'll feel the burdens lifting from your shoulders. God can truly give us contentment in our struggles. As II Corinthians 12:10 (THE VOICE) says, "I am at peace . . . in any weaknesses, insults, hardships, persecutions, and afflictions . . . because when I am at my weakest, He makes me strong."

We can also find peace and contentment in knowing the Lord is with us every step of the way in our challenging seasons. Whatever we are going through, we can trust that He is always watching over us. God's care for us and His presence with us are constant, and we have His assurance on that: "Never will I leave you; never will I forsake you" (Hebrews 13:5 NIV). This steadfast presence reminds us of the abundance and goodness He provides in every aspect of our lives. And that includes our time around the table, as we enjoy delicious food like this Veggie Crescent Pizza, filled with vibrant, flavorful ingredients.

As you enjoy this pizza for brunch or an afternoon snack, say a prayer of thanks to God for His care, provision, and the lasting contentment only He can provide—a contentment we can experience in every season.

> *You direct me on the path that leads to a beautiful life. As I walk with You, the pleasures are never-ending, and I know true joy and contentment.*
> **PSALM 16:11 THE VOICE**

> *God's goodness is the root of all goodness; and our goodness . . . springs out of His goodness.*
> **WILLIAM TYNDALE**

> *"Seek the Kingdom of God above all else . . . and He will give you everything you need."*
> **MATTHEW 6:33 NLT**

> *The fear of the Lord leads to life; then one rests content, untouched by trouble.*
> **PROVERBS 19:23 NIV**

> *God . . . richly provides us with everything.*
> **1 TIMOTHY 6:17 NIV**

> *A state of mind that sees God in everything is evidence of growth in grace and a thankful heart.*
> **CHARLES FINNEY**

veggie crescent pizza

This is a great recipe to make for brunch or a snack!

PREP: 40 MIN. | COOK: 15 MIN. | TOTAL TIME: 55 MIN. | SERVINGS: 16–20

- 2 (8-ounce) cans refrigerated crescent rolls
- 1 (8-ounce) package cream cheese, softened
- ¾ to 1 cup mayonnaise
- 1 (1-ounce) packet dry ranch dressing mix
- 1 cup broccoli, chopped
- 1 cup cucumber, chopped
- 1 cup tomato, chopped
- ½ cup carrots, shredded
- ½ cup green onions, chopped
- 1 cup shredded cheddar cheese

1. Preheat oven to 375°F. Set aside an ungreased 10 x 15-inch rimmed pan.

2. Unroll the 2 cans of crescent roll dough and separate into 4 rectangles. Press the dough into the bottom and up the sides of the 10 x 15-inch pan to form a crust. Bake for 13 to 15 minutes or until golden brown. Cool completely (or for at least 30 minutes).

3. While the crust is baking and cooling, chop the veggies and make the cream cheese filling. To make the filling, mix the cream cheese, mayonnaise, and dry ranch dressing mix together in a small bowl; set aside.
(**NOTE:** Start with ¾ cup mayonnaise, and if you want the filling creamier, you can add another ¼ cup.)

4. When the crust has cooled, spread the cream cheese mixture over it, then top with the broccoli, cucumber, tomato, carrots, and green onions. Sprinkle the cheddar cheese over everything. Chill for at least 30 minutes, then cut into squares and serve.

life-giving light

*"As long as I am in the world,
there is plenty of light.
I am the world's Light."*
JOHN 9:5 THE MESSAGE

The longer, brighter days of summer give everything in nature more life and energy. The sun shines in all its glory, and more sunlight means more growth for plants, flowers, and fruit. All growing things are drawn to the sunlight; it's life-giving for them and they need it every day to thrive. Most berry bushes, for example—like raspberries and blueberries—grow best in full sunlight. When they get the light they need, they're stronger, and they produce more fruit.

We need light to thrive in our faith too, but the light we need is the life-giving light that comes from God. Just as sunlight brings growth to plants, the light from God and His Word brings growth to us—in wisdom and strength. John 8:12 (THE VOICE) says, "If you walk with Me, you will thrive in the nourishing light that gives life and will not know darkness." God is the one true light (see John 1:9), and there is no darkness in Him at all (see I John 1:5). Darkness is the absence of light and brings fear, worry, and hopelessness, but God is light, and His radiant, powerful light can break through any darkness in our lives, filling us with peace and hope. God can work in any situation that seems impossible for us to get through, because *nothing* is impossible for Him. We can give our problems to Him as we pray and trust that He will work things out in the best way and in the right timing.

Here are some ways God's life-giving light can work in our lives:

- His light guides us. "Your word is a lamp to guide my feet and a light for my path" (Psalm 119:105 NLT).

- His light strengthens us. "We never give up. . . . Our inner strength in the Lord is growing every day" (II Corinthians 4:16 TLB).

- His light gives us wisdom and truth: "Open my eyes, so that I may see the wonderful truths in Your law" (Psalm 119:18 GNT).

- His light protects us. "The LORD is my light. . . . My fortress, protecting me from danger" (Psalm 27:1 NLT).

- His light gives us hope. "Shine Your light on the hope You are calling them to embrace" (Ephesians 1:18 THE VOICE).
- His light is always with us. "The LORD will be your everlasting light" (Isaiah 60:19 CSB).

As we enjoy the light-filled beauty of our summer days, let it be a reminder of the life-giving light God gives us. And let's take the time to enjoy the fruit of His light—like fresh, ripe berries! You can use them to make some easy Berry Tarts. Topped with blueberries and raspberries, these tarts can be enjoyed for brunch or an afternoon snack. As you arrange the berries on top of the tarts, thank God for the light He gives us to help us grow and stay strong, and for the many ways He guides and watches over us. Because of His light, we never have to live in darkness.

Lord, we're so grateful for Your powerful light that can chase away every bit of darkness in our lives. Because of the light of Your presence and the light of Your Word, we are filled with comfort, peace, and hope. They bring us the guidance, wisdom, and strength we need to get through our tough days and busy seasons. Thank You for being the lamp that lights our way, letting us see things clearly even in the most confusing of times. Thank You for the way Your light surrounds us and protects us, keeping us safe in Your care—it reminds us that there is never a moment when You are not with us. We praise You because Your light and love in our lives is everlasting, and no darkness will ever be able to overcome them. You are the Light of the world, and we are overwhelmed by Your goodness, kindness, and faithfulness to us. They are never-ending—just like the timelessness of Your holy and righteous light. Amen.

berry tarts

This recipe uses fresh blueberries and raspberries. You can use other kinds of fresh fruit to top the tarts, including sliced strawberries, blackberries, sliced kiwifruit, and sliced peaches.

PREP: 25 MIN. | COOK: 0 MIN. | TOTAL TIME: 25 MIN. | SERVINGS: 6

1 (8-ounce) package cream cheese, softened

½ cup powdered sugar

¼ teaspoon pure vanilla extract

6 dessert shells

Raspberry or blueberry jam (½ teaspoon per tart)

Fresh blueberries and raspberries

1. Make the filling: In a medium-size bowl, mix together the softened cream cheese and powdered sugar until smooth. Add the vanilla extract, blending everything together well; set aside.

2. Arrange the dessert shells on a serving plate. Spread ½ teaspoon jam onto the bottom of each dessert shell, then add 1⅓ tablespoons of the cream cheese mixture over the jam.

3. Top each filled tart with the fresh blueberries and raspberries. Have fun making different fruit arrangements on the top of each tart!

4. Refrigerate tarts until ready to serve.

take a break

"I'll refresh tired bodies;
I'll restore tired souls."
JEREMIAH 31:25 THE MESSAGE

Even though summer is typically a slower season, life can still be busy. There are vacations to plan, family reunions to organize, and garage sales to get ready for, on top of all the other things at home and work. No wonder we feel like we need a break! We all need time to recharge and be refreshed. Taking a break from our busyness is something that's good for us to do. We can follow the example Jesus gives us in Mark 6, when a large crowd of people gathered where He and His disciples were. "There were so many people coming and going that Jesus and His disciples didn't even have time to eat. So He said to them, 'Let us go off by ourselves to some place where we will be alone and you can rest a while'" (Mark 6:31 GNT). The disciples, traveling in pairs, had just returned from their first mission trips, and now they were surrounded by a crowd of people, not having had any time to eat. Jesus knew they needed to take a break and rest. Have you had days like that too, when you were so busy, you hardly had time to eat or do much of anything for yourself? In times like that, you need a break from all the busyness around you.

Just as Jesus knew it would be good for His disciples to have a break, He knows it's good for us to rest and unwind, and He wants that kind of refreshment for us. Taking a break could be as simple as going for a walk and praying. Or taking a tea or coffee break and reading your Bible. Maybe you're needing to have some time that's calm and quiet—time to just sit and be with Jesus. Simple things like these can renew and recharge us, and then, like the psalmist, we can say: "My soul has become calm, quiet, and contented in You" (Psalm 131:2 THE VOICE).

Maybe you and your family, or some of your friends, could use a break. Spending some relaxing time together can be a time of refreshment for everyone. It could be a casual meal, like a simple picnic, in the backyard. Or just a time of sharing light snacks and praying together. Taking time to encourage each other can be so reviving. Something simple to make for get-togethers like these is Stuffed Ranch Eggs, hard-boiled eggs filled with a savory egg yolk filling. If you don't have time to hard-boil your eggs, just use packages of eggs that are already hard-boiled and peeled. As you enjoy this easy-to-make appetizer and snack, whether it's time just for you or with others, let it be a reminder of how restoring it can be to take a break and find refreshment in quiet moments with the Lord.

Restore the joy of Your salvation to me,
and sustain me.
PSALM 51:12 CSB

The God of all grace . . .
will Himself restore you and make you strong.
1 PETER 5:10 NIV

Rest time is not waste time.
It is economy to gather fresh strength. . . .
It is wisdom to take occasional furlough.
In the long run, we shall do more by sometimes doing less.
CHARLES SPURGEON

God is my strength;
He is all I ever need.
PSALM 73:26 GNT

*I will say of the L*ORD,
"He is my refuge and my fortress,
my God, in whom I trust."
PSALM 91:2 NIV

Make it your goal to lead a peaceful life.
1 THESSALONIANS 4:11 THE VOICE

stuffed ranch eggs

No time to hard-boil the eggs? Just use two packages of six eggs that are already hard-boiled and peeled.

PREP: 50 MIN. | COOK: 10 MIN. | TOTAL TIME: 60 MIN. | SERVINGS: 12 (24 HALVES)

12 hard-boiled eggs, peeled

3 teaspoons dry ranch dressing mix, from a 1-ounce package

6 tablespoons mayonnaise

2 teaspoons prepared yellow mustard

Dash of salt and pepper, to taste

Optional: Paprika, for sprinkling on top

Optional: Chopped fresh chives, for sprinkling on top (about 1½ tablespoons)

1. Cut hard-boiled, peeled eggs lengthwise in half.
2. Remove the yolks from the egg whites and place yolks in a small-to medium-size bowl; mash them with a fork.
3. Add the dry ranch dressing mix, mayonnaise, and mustard to the bowl with the mashed yolks. Add a dash of salt and pepper, if desired. Mix everything together well, until smooth and creamy.
4. Fill egg white halves with the egg yolk mixture.
5. Sprinkle with paprika and/or chopped chives, if desired, and refrigerate for 30 minutes to 1 hour before serving.

He cares and provides

*"You have a Father caring for you,
a Father who knows all your needs."*
LUKE 12:30 THE VOICE

As lovely as summer weather is, sometimes there can be periods of "drought" when the temperatures are high. During this time, plants may wither in the intense heat. In the same way, when we're going through challenging, drought-like times in our lives, it can wither our spirits. These times of lack or hardship can fill us with worry and leave us feeling discouraged. Maybe the lack many of us have is a lack of time to get things done! Whatever our situation, we crave replenishment, and we can't get it on our own.

A passage in the gospel of Luke reminds us that God is the only One who can provide all our needs: "Think about those beautiful wild lilies growing over there. They don't work up a sweat toiling for needs or wants—they don't worry about clothing. Yet the great King Solomon never had an outfit that was half as glorious as theirs! . . . How much more you can depend on God to care for you . . . . Don't let your mind be filled with anxiety" (Luke 12:27–29 THE VOICE). God cares so completely for His creation, and He cares *so much more* for us. Whether our needs are for security, safety, food, clothing (see Luke 12:31), or *anything*, we can come to Him in prayer and ask Him to provide.

God wants us to come to Him daily for our needs. He is our loving Father, and He wants to care for us every single day. When we pray the Lord's Prayer, we ask Him to "give us today our daily bread" (Matthew 6:11 NIV). Asking for "daily bread" means asking for our needs to be met, not just for food but for any of our everyday essentials. We can trust that He will provide what we need every day, day after day. Sometimes He may not provide in the way we are hoping for, but He will always provide for us in the way that's best for us.

There are reminders of God's blessings all around us in the simplest of everyday things: the couch we relax on, the clothes in our closet, and the food in our pantry. Maybe part of our "daily bread" is that bag of potatoes in our kitchen. With those simple, basic potatoes we can make delicious Classic Potato Salad. When you prepare the potatoes and mix in the creamy dressing and other ingredients, take time to think about all the ways God shows His care and provides for your every need. Let's thank Him for being such a good, loving Father to us!

Lord, You are such a loving, caring Father, and we thank You and praise You for all the ways You provide for us. We see how You care so completely for Your creation, and You've told us in Your Word that You care so much more for us! No matter what we are lacking, You fill every single need. You care for us so lovingly, from our biggest, most overwhelming requests to the smallest of our needs. That is a comforting reminder to us that we are seen, heard, and loved by You. Help us to remember that, because You take care of us so well, there is no need for us to worry or be anxious about anything. All we need to do is come to You. We're so grateful for the ways You provide for us every single day, in every way. You're always faithful to bless us with exactly what we need, and even more than we need, because You are a kind and generous Father. We love You so much. Amen.

classic potato salad

Time-saving tips: Boil the potatoes and the eggs at the same time, in different pots. They both take ten to fifteen minutes to cook. You can also mix the dressing ingredients together and chop the onion and celery while the potatoes and eggs are cooking and cooling.

PREP: 45 MIN. | COOK: 15 MIN. | TOTAL TIME: 60 MIN. | SERVINGS: 6–8

3 pounds potatoes, peeled and cut into ¾-inch cubes

1 to 1¼ cups mayonnaise (use 1¼ cups for a creamier potato salad)

1 teaspoon sugar

½ tablespoon vinegar

1 teaspoon yellow mustard

½ teaspoon salt

¼ teaspoon ground pepper

¼ cup sweet pickle relish

⅔ cup onion, finely chopped

2 celery ribs, chopped

4 hard-boiled eggs, chopped

Paprika, for garnish

1. Place peeled and cubed potatoes in a large saucepan, covering with water (add some salt to the water). Bring to a boil. Reduce heat, then simmer and cook until potato cubes are tender, about 10 minutes.

2. Drain potatoes and let cool to room temperature.

3. In a large bowl, mix the mayonnaise, sugar, vinegar, mustard, salt, and pepper, blending well.

4. Add the cubed potatoes, pickle relish, onion, and celery; stir and toss gently until all ingredients are coated with the mayonnaise mixture. Gently stir in the chopped eggs.

5. Cover and refrigerate until chilled. When ready to serve, garnish the potato salad with a sprinkle of paprika.

never stop blooming

**Kindness, peace, love—
may they never stop blooming
in you and from you.**
JUDE 1:2 THE VOICE

It's always nice to receive a letter or a card from a family member or friend with an encouraging message, isn't it? Some of the books of the New Testament are actually letters that were written by the apostles to bless, encourage, and teach the believers in the early church. Jude wrote early on in his letter in Jude 1:2 (NLT), "May God give you more and more mercy, peace, and love." He was asking God to bless the readers of his letter with an abundance of His mercy (or kindness), peace, and love . . . *more and more*, in ever-increasing amounts. What a wonderful blessing! These blessings from God are meant for us to receive too.

God demonstrates His mercy, peace, and love to us every day as we see Him work in our circumstances. He shows us His *mercy* through His kindness and compassion. When we're going through challenging times, we have the confidence of knowing He will bring us the help and the comfort we need: "God's mercy is so abundant, and His love for us is so great" (Ephesians 2:4 GNT). God's *peace* gives us an inner calmness. The peace He gives us is *perfect* peace, keeping us strong and steady as we trust in Him. "You will keep in perfect peace all who trust in You" (Isaiah 26:3 NLT). And God's *love* for us is unconditional, immeasurable, and everlasting. We don't have to do anything to earn His love; He loves us just because we're us, and we feel secure in His love. "I have always loved you, so I continue to show you My constant love" (Jeremiah 31:3 GNT). As we experience God's abundant mercy, peace, and love in our lives, we grow in our faith. And as we grow, we are better able to reflect His kindness, peace, and love to others.

As we continue to experience God's kindness, peace, and love, they bloom *in* us, and then *from* us. And as we continue to grow and draw near to Him, *they will never stop blooming in us and from us*. Because of that, we can demonstrate God's kindness, peace, and love to others, helping them see the abundance of His grace and goodness.

Today's recipe was chosen to reflect God's abundant blessings, with baby spinach, romaine lettuce, strawberries, cucumbers, and a variety of nourishing and tasty ingredients coming together to create a beautiful and delicious salad. As you slice the strawberries and veggies, think about all the ways God has blessed your life with His mercy, peace, and love and who you can share His love with. And say a prayer of thanks that His abundant supply of goodness never runs out!

In His great mercy He has given us new birth into a living hope through the resurrection of Jesus Christ.
I PETER 1:3 NIV

Let us then approach God's throne of grace with confidence, so that we may receive mercy and find grace to help us in our time of need.
HEBREWS 4:16 NIV

May you have the power to understand . . . how wide, how long, how high, and how deep His love is.
EPHESIANS 3:18 NLT

There is not a flower that opens, not a seed that falls into the ground, and not an ear of wheat that nods on the end of its stalk in the wind that does not preach and proclaim the greatness and the mercy of God to the whole world.
BILLY GRAHAM

He will take delight in you with gladness. With His love, He will calm all your fears. He will rejoice over you with joyful songs.
ZEPHANIAH 3:17 NLT

The Lord blesses His people with peace.
PSALM 29:11 NIV

strawberry spinach salad

This salad is like summer in a bowl! If you don't have feta cheese on hand, you can substitute your favorite shredded cheese.

PREP: 20 MIN. | COOK: 0 MIN. | TOTAL TIME: 20 MIN. | SERVINGS: 8

4 cups fresh baby spinach leaves

4 cups romaine lettuce, chopped

2 cups strawberries, sliced

1 cup cucumber, sliced

¾ cup red onion, thinly sliced

½ cup sliced almonds, divided

½ cup crumbled feta cheese, divided

½ cup bottled strawberry balsamic vinaigrette

1. In a large bowl, add spinach, lettuce, sliced strawberries, sliced cucumber, sliced red onion, and all but 2 tablespoons of the sliced almonds and feta cheese (save the 2 tablespoons each of almonds and cheese for sprinkling on top of the salad).

2. Toss all the ingredients together well.

3. When ready to serve, drizzle salad with the strawberry vinaigrette and toss gently. Then sprinkle the top of the salad with the remaining feta cheese and sliced almonds. Serve immediately.

4. If serving a little later, stop after Step #2 and refrigerate the salad until ready to serve. Just before serving, toss in the dressing and sprinkle the top of the salad with the remaining feta cheese and sliced almonds.

calm in the storm

> He said to the waves, "Be still!"
> The wind died down,
> and there was a great calm.
>
> MARK 4:39 GNT

As we get further into summer, a light rainfall can be a welcome relief from the heat. Listening to the soft patter of raindrops can even be relaxing. But thunderstorms are a different matter. The lightning, thunder, strong winds, and pelting rain can all be a little unnerving. These storms often develop quickly, too, with the weather changing from bright and sunny to dark and stormy in a short amount of time, so we need shelter to protect us in the storm.

Storms in our lives can be a lot like the ones we see outside. The "storms" we face are the difficult or discouraging things that come our way, and many times, they are hardships that can catch us by surprise. They're often unexpected or happen quickly. And they might bring us worry or fear as we're caught in them. We need a "shelter" during times like these to keep our hearts and minds at peace as we go through the storm.

In Mark 4:37–39 (GNT), Jesus showed His disciples that they could trust Him to calm the storms in their lives as they crossed the Sea of Galilee in the boat with Him: "Suddenly a strong wind blew up, and the waves began to spill over into the boat, so that it was about to fill with water. Jesus was in the back of the boat, sleeping with His head on a pillow. The disciples woke Him up and said, 'Teacher, don't You care that we are about to die?' Jesus stood up and commanded the wind, 'Be quiet!' and He said to the waves, 'Be still!' The wind died down, and there was a great calm." When the dangerous storm developed, the disciples feared for their lives. They asked, "Don't You care, Jesus?" We ask Him the same question: "Don't You care about what I'm going through?" In difficult situations, we may wonder if God cares or if He's forgotten about us. Jesus showed His disciples that He *did* care and that He could calm any storm they would ever go through. He can do the same for us when we call out to Him. Sometimes He may calm the storm, and sometimes He may walk through the storm with us. There are times when God allows us to go through storms to grow our faith. Whatever He does, we can know He will always be our "shelter" in the storm, giving us His peace and protection.

Sometimes the best thing we can do during a thunderstorm when we're safe inside at home is to make something comforting to eat, like Taco Pasta Salad. It's a delicious blend of ground beef, pasta, veggies, and cheese. As you cook the beef and pasta and toss all the tasty ingredients together, recall how God was with you in your most recent "storm." May this dish remind you of the comfort and protection God is faithful to bring during every storm you face.

Lord, we thank You for being our Protector and Shelter in the storms of life. And we are grateful for Your Word and all the wisdom and truth we learn from it. It teaches us that You know and care about the difficult days and seasons we experience, that You are always with us, and that there is always hope, no matter how dangerous any storm may seem. There will never be a storm that is too difficult for You to get us through. Help us to stay strong and confident in the face of whatever might bring us fear, knowing that whatever we go through, You never, ever forget about us or leave us. Let us always remember that You are, and always will be, our refuge and ever-present help in anything we face. And we thank You that, even in the midst of difficulties, You can use those situations to build our faith and trust in You as You carry us through them. We love You and thank You for surrounding us with Your perfect peace and care. Amen.

taco pasta salad

You can also add sliced black olives or black beans to this salad. And using pre-shredded lettuce from a bag saves lots of time.

PREP: 20 MIN. | COOK: 15 MIN. | TOTAL TIME: 35 MIN. | SERVINGS: 6

- 2 cups rotini (spiral) pasta, uncooked
- 1 pound lean ground beef
- 1 (1-ounce) packet taco seasoning
- ¾ cup red bell pepper (about 1 medium), diced
- ¾ cup green onions (about 4), sliced
- 3/4 cup frozen corn kernels, thawed
- 3 cups lettuce, shredded
- 3 cups cherry tomatoes
- 2 cups shredded Mexican blend cheese
- ¾ cup Catalina dressing
- For garnish (optional): chopped cilantro, sour cream, avocado
- Tortilla chips

1. Cook the pasta according to package directions, then drain and rinse in cold water; set aside.
2. In a large skillet, cook beef, breaking into crumbles, over medium heat until no longer pink. Drain excess fat. Stir in the taco seasoning.
3. In a large bowl, stir the pasta and ground beef together. Then add the bell pepper, green onions, corn, lettuce, cherry tomatoes, and cheese.
4. Toss everything together, then add the Catalina dressing and toss to coat all the ingredients.
5. If desired, garnish the pasta salad with sliced or chopped avocado, chopped cilantro, and/or a large dollop of sour cream. Serve with tortilla chips.

true freedom

**Freedom is what we have—
Christ has set us free!**

GALATIANS 5:1 GNT

Every summer, Americans celebrate the many freedoms we have in our country on Independence Day with parades, cookouts, flag-waving, and festive fireworks. It's a day filled with fun and excitement as well as a time of reflection and gratitude for the freedoms we enjoy—including freedom of religion, freedom of speech, and freedom of the press. And it's a time when we remember those in the military who have served and are serving our country, sacrificing so much to keep us free.

As grateful as we are for the freedoms we have in our country, there's another freedom we have that means so much more: the *true* freedom we have in Jesus when we invite Him into our hearts. "In any heart where the Spirit of the Lord is present, there is liberty" (II Corinthians 3:17 THE VOICE). Through Jesus' sacrifice on the cross and His resurrection, He set us free from the power of sin and death. "For those who belong to Christ Jesus . . . the power of the life-giving Spirit has freed you" (Romans 8:1–2 NLT). That is what true freedom is all about!

This freedom we have because of Jesus also means we can be free of the weight of past wrongs, mistakes, and regrets. We can release all those things to Him. It means that, as we grow closer to Him, we have the freedom to live the abundant life He wants for us, free from worry and filled with joy. When we look to God and follow His leading, we can be confident that our heavenly Father knows—much more than we know ourselves—what's best for us. And that gives us the freedom to move forward, discovering all the blessings He wants to fill our lives with. True freedom is living the flourishing, abundant life Jesus promises us—a life of joy, peace, and fulfilment. There's always a chance that the freedoms of this world can be taken away, but the true freedom that Jesus gives to us is ours forever!

As you plan your Independence Day celebration, you may want to include these fun and festive cookies as a special treat. As you go through the steps of the recipe—lining the baking sheet, melting the chocolate chips, and adding the sprinkles—try to keep your thoughts and heart focused on how thankful you are to Jesus for setting you free. That is something to truly celebrate!

*"If you hear My voice and abide in My word . . .
you will know the truth,
and that truth will give you freedom."*
JOHN 8:31-32 THE VOICE

*May we think of freedom,
not as the right to do as we please,
but as the opportunity to do what is right.*
PETER MARSHALL

*You have been given freedom . . .
freedom to love and serve each other.*
GALATIANS 5:13 TLB

*It is by believing in your heart
that you are made right with God,
and it is by openly declaring your faith
that you are saved.*
ROMANS 10:10 NLT

*If you believe on
the Lord Jesus Christ you are free.*
DWIGHT L. MOODY

*I will walk in freedom,
for I have devoted myself
to Your commandments.*
PSALM 119:45 NLT

easy patriotic cookies

After decorating these cookies, you'll want to chill them in the refrigerator for at least thirty minutes before serving to let the chocolate set.

PREP: 35 MIN. | COOK: 0 MIN. | TOTAL TIME: 35 MIN. | SERVINGS: 36–40

- 2 (4-ounce) white or semisweet chocolate baking bars, coarsely chopped (or use 1 of each but melt them separately)
- Red, white, and blue sprinkles (use one kind or several different kinds)
- 36 to 40 of your favorite purchased or homemade smaller-sized cookies (shortbread, oatmeal, chocolate chip, peanut butter, chocolate sandwich cookies . . . whatever you like!)

1. Line a large baking sheet with parchment paper or waxed paper; set aside.
2. Melt the chopped chocolate in a microwave-safe bowl, heating for 30 seconds; remove and stir, then heat in 15-second increments, stopping and stirring after each time until the chocolate is smooth.
3. Dip each cookie into the melted chocolate about halfway; gently shake off excess chocolate, then sprinkle the chocolate with the red, white, and blue sprinkles.
4. Place dipped and sprinkled cookies on lined baking sheet to let chocolate set. It will set more quickly if you place the sheet of cookies in the refrigerator for at least a half hour.
5. Serve cookies when chocolate is set or put them in an airtight container and keep refrigerated until ready to serve.

beautifully transformed

Do not allow this world to mold you in its own image. Instead, be transformed from the inside out by renewing your mind.
ROMANS 12:2 THE VOICE

The slower pace of summer gives us a welcome change from the busy routines of other seasons. In these longer, light-filled days, we see beautiful transformation all around us. Caterpillars are now butterflies; flower buds are now blossoms. These can be reminders of how God is doing a transforming work in our own lives and what He's teaching us. As we follow Jesus, God wants to reshape us, and we can grow in beautiful ways by being open to the new things He wants to do in us and in our lives. Romans 12:2 (NIV) says, "Do not conform to the pattern of this world, but be transformed by the renewing of your mind." We are not to be molded by the world around us, but instead be transformed and shaped into the person God created us to be. He can transform our lives and renew our minds "from the inside out," changing our attitudes and the way we think so that our hearts, minds, and spirits are aligned with His good plans for our lives.

The moment we accept Christ into our hearts, His transformative work begins. It's a deep, heart-changing process that affects how we see ourselves, how we relate to others, and how we walk through life. We start thinking differently—no longer focusing on earthly concerns, but on what eternity in heaven looks like. And ultimately, we discover that it's all about becoming more and more like our heavenly Father and growing closer to Him. "Put on your new nature, and be renewed as you learn to know your Creator and become like Him" (Colossians 3:10 NLT).

The beautiful transformation God can do in each of us is not a onetime event; it's a continual, lifelong process. He continues to transform us season by season and day by day. As we travel this journey, we may stumble or get off track. But because of God's love and grace, we can get right back on His perfect path for our lives and continue to move ahead, step by step, as He guides our way.

Today's recipe mirrors God's transformative work in our hearts. Just like this Peach Cobbler Cake, which begins as a mix of different ingredients, His work in us combines all the parts of our lives, bringing them together to create something beautiful and sweet in the end. When you take it out of the oven, you'll see the transformation—a dessert full of peachy summer flavor! As you enjoy this easy-to-make cake, think about some of the transforming work God has done in your own life. In what ways have you grown? Let's thank Him for the beautiful transformation He brings to our lives every day!

Lord, it's amazing to see Your transforming work in nature every season, and it's even more amazing to know You are doing a transforming work in us. Help us to be open to all that You want to teach us and all the ways You want to shape us. Give us the desire and strength to let go of the ways of the world—anything that holds us back from all You want us to be—and hold fast to Your ways. Work inside of us so our hearts and minds will be aligned with Your truth, Your ways, and Your purposes. Give us discernment and wisdom to follow the path You have for us and to be obedient to how You are leading us. Help us grow to be more and more like You each day. We thank You and praise You for all the good ways You are working inside of us and in our lives. Amen.

peach cobbler cake

Top this easy and delicious cake with whipped cream or a scoop of vanilla ice cream.

PREP: 15 MIN. | COOK: 40 MIN. | TOTAL TIME: 55 MIN. | SERVINGS: 12

- 2 (15-ounce) cans sliced peaches in light syrup
- 2½ tablespoons light brown sugar
- ¾ teaspoon ground cinnamon
- 1 (15.25-ounce) package yellow cake mix
- ⅔ cup pecans, coarsely chopped
- ⅔ cup (or 11 tablespoons) cold butter

1. Preheat oven to 350°F degrees. Grease or spray a 9 x 13-inch pan or baking dish.
2. Pour 1 can of sliced peaches, along with the light syrup, into the greased baking pan. Drain the second can of peaches and add them to the baking pan.
3. Sprinkle the light brown sugar and cinnamon evenly over the peaches in the pan. Then sprinkle the dry cake mix and chopped pecans evenly over everything.
4. Slice the cold butter into very thin slices, then place them evenly on top of the dry cake mix and chopped pecans.
5. Bake for 38 to 40 minutes, until top is golden. Tastes best served warm.

living with purpose

**It's in Christ that we find out who we are and what we are living for.
Long before we first heard of Christ . . .
He had His eye on us, had designs on us for glorious living.**

EPHESIANS 1:11 THE MESSAGE

We all have a special purpose. God wants to accomplish amazing things through each one of us! He formed incredible plans for our lives before we were even born. We are all intentionally created by God for a purpose—a purpose only we can fulfill with our own unique talents, abilities, and giftings. We are each created to be "one of a kind" and to play our unique role in God's beautiful plan.

To know our purpose, we need to look to God and His Word, because *it's in Christ that we find out who we are and what we are living for*. Only He can show us the purpose and plans He has for us. And we discover those plans as we read the Bible and pray for His wisdom and direction. He will always show us the right way to go: "You reveal the path of life to me; in Your presence is abundant joy" (Psalm 16:11 CSB).

Not only do we each have a special God-given purpose for our lives, God even determined the time in history we would live in and where we would live, to accomplish our purpose (see Acts 17:26). That's how loved and important we are to Him. He's given us a special purpose that can make a difference in the lives of others and glorify Him, at just the right time, exactly where He has placed us. And whatever purpose God is calling us to fulfill, we can trust that He will equip us for it. He tells us, "I set you apart before you were born. . . . I will be with you" (Jeremiah 1:5, 8 CSB). We never have to hesitate about moving forward in the purpose God has given us, because He will provide us with everything we need as we step out in faith.

For some of us, our purpose may be serving our community in some way, caring for our family, or sharing God's love and truth with others in our workplace. God's purposes for us are as unique and individual as we are. We can know without a doubt that, as we look to Him, He will never fail to guide us into His perfect plan and purpose for our lives.

If you are struggling to find your "purpose," take some time today to ask God if you are aligned with His plan for your life. Pray, listen, read His Word, and maybe even ask a trusted mentor. And then, be open to hearing what might be next for you, no matter how far-fetched it sounds. Remember, He has far more for you than you could possibly dream or imagine (Ephesians 3:20).

When you make today's recipe for Chocolate Mint Brownies, be reminded that God's plans for you are sweet, refreshing, and oh-so good!

> *God can do anything, you know—far more than you could ever imagine or guess or request in your wildest dreams! He does it not by pushing us around but by working within us, His Spirit deeply and gently within us.*
> **EPHESIANS 3:20–21 THE MESSAGE**

> *It is God who works in you to will and to act in order to fulfill His good purpose.*
> **PHILIPPIANS 2:13 NIV**

> *If you wish to know God, you must know His Word. If you wish to perceive His power, you must see how He works by His Word. If you wish to know His purpose before it comes to pass, you can only discover it by His Word.*
> **CHARLES SPURGEON**

> *"They are My own people, and I created them to bring Me glory."*
> **ISAIAH 43:7 GNT**

> *The Lord will fulfill His purpose for me.*
> **PSALM 138:8 CSB**

> *God is faithful and in His faithfulness called you out into an intimate relationship with His Son, our Lord Jesus.*
> **I CORINTHIANS 1:9 THE VOICE**

chocolate mint brownies

The rich, minty flavor of these brownies makes them such a refreshing dessert. You'd never know they were made with brownie mix!

PREP: 20 MIN. | COOK: 35 MIN. | TOTAL TIME: 55 MIN. | SERVINGS: 9

FOR BROWNIES:

1 (18-ounce) box brownie mix, plus water, oil, and eggs to use as directed on box

⅔ cup mint chocolate chips (**NOTE:** you'll need a total of 1 cup; ⅓ cup will be used for sprinkling on top)

FOR FROSTING:

⅓ cup butter, softened

4 ounces (half an 8-ounce block) cream cheese, softened

3 cups powdered sugar

1 tablespoon milk

½ teaspoon mint extract

5 to 10 drops green food coloring, or enough to get desired color

⅓ cup mint chocolate chips for sprinkling on top

Optional: green sprinkles

1. Preheat oven to 350°F. Line a 9 x 9-inch baking pan with parchment paper, letting edges of the paper go beyond the edges of the pan by 1 inch so you can lift brownies out after baking. Set aside.

2. In a large bowl, mix brownie batter as directed on box. After mixing, fold in ⅔ cup mint chocolate chips. Pour batter evenly into prepared pan.

3. Bake for 33 to 36 minutes, until toothpick inserted in center comes out clean or almost clean. Cool brownies completely before frosting.

4. While brownies are cooling, make the frosting: Blend the softened butter and cream cheese, then add the powdered sugar, milk, mint extract, and enough green food coloring for desired shade, mixing until smooth.

5. When brownies are completely cooled, spread frosting over them and sprinkle the ⅓ cup mint chocolate chips over the frosting. If desired, you can also sprinkle with green sprinkles. Cut into bars or squares.

THE CHANGING SEASONS:
summer-fall

The morning air feels a little more crisp as summer gently tumbles into fall. It's a reminder that the relaxing, barefoot days of this season are coming to an end. But we can still carry with us the joy and memories of how God has blessed our summer, like the colorful vibrance of the season, with all of creation so full of life and growth, and the early morning sunrises that reminded us of God's mercies, new every morning. Or how we discovered life lessons all around us in nature—the importance of being strongly rooted and secure in God's care, our need for His life-giving light to thrive, and the beautiful ways He works to bring transformation to our lives. We took some much-needed breaks whenever we could to refresh our souls, and we saw that God was and always will be our loving Provider and Protector during storms and times of drought. And we continue to be encouraged in knowing that God has given us a special purpose that's as unique as He created us to be.

Our special memories of summer may still linger as we move forward into the cooler fall season, but soon we'll be embracing all the things we love about autumn: the mums that bloom bold and beautiful, the colorful leaves that gradually drift to the ground, and the quiet beauty of the first frost. It's a busier season, with school starting, hayrides to go on, and pumpkin patches to visit. We wrap ourselves in cozy sweaters, cheer on our favorite football teams, and sip on mugs of hot apple cider and pumpkin lattes. And in the longer evenings, we spend more time in the coziness of our homes, enjoying meals and conversation around the table.

Fall is also a season of harvest—a time of gathering, celebration, and gratitude, when we're especially mindful of all the ways God provides for us. Psalm 67:5–6 (THE VOICE) says, "May the people praise You with their whole hearts, O God; may every man, woman, and child on the earth praise You. The land has supplied a bountiful harvest, and the True God, our God, has poured out His blessings to us all." In this season and every season, let's always remember to praise Him with all of our hearts and be grateful for the many ways He blesses us. He gives us a bountiful harvest, and that harvest is not just the food we have on our table, but also all the other ways He cares and provides for us. Let's overflow with thankfulness to God as we enter this season of harvest and celebrate all that He is and all that He so generously gives.

Lord, we are so grateful for all the joy and growth we experienced in our summer season—for all we learned from You and Your Word. We're thankful for the true freedom we have and the abundant life that is ours because of You. We praise You for all the ways You work in our lives, for the many ways You bless us, and for how completely You care for us. As we look to the fall season, we thank You for the harvest of blessings that come from Your hand. You are always so faithful to provide for our needs. We ask that You give our families good health in the cooler months of autumn. Let us feel Your presence with us each day and also as we gather together to celebrate Your grace and goodness to us. In the busyness of this season, help us to keep our focus on You and how You are guiding us. Let our lives always be glorifying and honoring to You. Amen.

fall

*They sowed the fields and planted grapevines
and reaped an abundant harvest.*

PSALM 107:37 GNT

Sometimes we call fall the golden season, as the landscape becomes rich with warm yellows, oranges, and reds—the last burst of color we will see for the year before trees gently let go of their leaves. We also call it the harvest season because it's the time of year when many crops are ready to be gathered. All of the hard work we put into those seedlings last season are now blooming. We see orchards filled with crisp apples and soft, ripe pears, and fields full of grain ready for picking. Pumpkins start to appear on porches and in our favorite treats. There's other harvest bounty too: squash, kale, leeks, and potatoes. So many good things to savor!

Fall is the time of year when we celebrate God's goodness to us—the abundance of His blessings and His faithfulness to supply all our needs. It's a time when we're reminded to have a heart of gratitude, giving thanks to the Lord for all He is and all He does. There's so much to thank Him for right where we're at in the present, and we can continue to hold on to His promises that He will take care of us in the future: "I will be your God through all your lifetime. . . . I made you and I will care for you" (Isaiah 46:4 TLB).

This fall, let's celebrate the harvest with joy and thanksgiving, as God surrounds us with His love, kindness, and care. And let's trust in Him fully and completely, believing that He "will indeed give what is good" (Psalm 85:12 NIV).

lessons from the trees

He has made everything beautiful in its time.

ECCLESIASTES 3:11 NIV

It's time to welcome fall! We love all the color and beauty this season brings and how nature reflects the artistry of its Creator. "One generation after another will celebrate Your great works. . . . Your majesty and glorious splendor have captivated me; I will meditate on Your wonders" (Psalm 145:4–5 THE VOICE). As we enter the fall season, we can learn some helpful lessons from God's creation—like the changes in the trees and their leaves. They give us a new perspective about how beautiful change can be and how freeing it is to let go of unnecessary things.

As we watch the tree leaves turn from summer greens to a patchwork of warm and vivid colors, it reminds us that circumstances and seasons in our lives may change, but God can bring beauty out of every change we go through. There are times when change isn't easy, but through it, God can lead us into new experiences and opportunities that grow us, bless us, and draw us closer into the plans and purposes He has for us. We can embrace change because it's a process where He is beautifully transforming us to become more like Him. As He does this work of transformation and change in us and in His creation, He makes "everything beautiful in its time" (Ecclesiastes 3:11 NIV).

There's more change later in the season as trees gracefully let go of their leaves. It's necessary for trees to release the weight of their leaves to keep their branches strong during the winter season and prepare for new growth in the spring. This helps us understand the importance of "letting go." Trees need to let go of their leaves to stay strong and grow. We need to let go of things for the same reason. Many times, we hold on to extra baggage from past seasons—memories, habits, or worries that weigh us down and keep us from moving forward into the new season of growth that God has for us. Like the trees, we also need to *let go* so we can stay strong and grow. What is it that you need to let go of today? What are you holding on to? Maybe you don't trust God is going to actually do anything about it. Maybe you are holding on to it to punish yourself when God has already forgiven you. Or maybe you think the only way to make things right is to hold a grudge. Ask God what you are holding on to that you no longer need to carry. Ask Him to help you surrender it all. He can free you from the weight of your burdens. Only when you release these will you be ready for new growth in the seasons ahead.

What better way to embrace this season of change than by starting your fall day with the warm, comforting flavors of Apple-Cheddar Biscuits? These easy-to-make drop biscuits are great served with eggs or just on their own.

*For in Him we live
and move and are!*
ACTS 17:28 TLB

*You can endure change
by pondering His permanence.*
MAX LUCADO

*Let the fields be jubilant,
and everything in them;
let all the trees of the forest sing for joy.*
PSALM 96:12 NIV

There is no growth without change.
RICK WARREN

*Nothing in all creation
is hidden from God's sight.*
HEBREWS 4:13 NIV

*Faith is confidence in what we hope for and
assurance about what we do not see.*
HEBREWS 11:1 NIV

apple-cheddar biscuits

The tart, grated apple makes these drop biscuits moist and tender!

PREP: 25 MIN. | COOK: 20 MIN. | TOTAL TIME: 45 MIN. | SERVINGS: 12

- 2 cups all-purpose baking mix
- ½ cup milk
- ½ teaspoon salt
- 1 cup coarsely grated Granny Smith apple, about 1 large
- 1⅓ cups shredded cheddar cheese
- 2 tablespoons finely chopped fresh chives, divided
- 2 tablespoons butter, melted

1. Preheat oven to 400°F. Line a 10 x 15-inch baking sheet with parchment paper; set aside.

2. In a large bowl, mix together the baking mix, milk, and salt. Then stir in the grated apple, shredded cheddar cheese, and 1 tablespoon of the chives, mixing until all ingredients are combined. (Save the rest of the chives for later.)

3. Drop dough by ¼ cup-fuls, about 2 inches apart, onto the parchment-lined baking sheet. (You can also use a scoop to drop the dough.)

4. Bake biscuits for 15 minutes. While baking the biscuits, mix the melted butter and remaining 1 tablespoon of chopped chives together.

5. Remove biscuits from oven and brush the tops with the butter/chive mixture, then return to the oven to bake an additional 4 to 5 minutes, until biscuits are golden. Serve warm.

enjoying cozy comforts

"My purpose is to give them a rich and satisfying life."
JOHN 10:10 NLT

The crisp air of fall mornings greets us as we walk out the door, and we immediately want to sit on the front porch swing, snuggle in a warm blanket, and sip on hot cider, tea, or coffee. But let's face it, who has time for these simple joys? The world is waiting—we have kids to drop off, presentations to deliver, and groceries to pick up. So how can we embrace the fall season when there's no time for a hot drink or a good book? A few simple touches of fall decor in your home can serve as a constant reminder of the season's warmth. Even as you rush out the door, a bowl of fall fruit or a cozy accent can prompt you to pause and enjoy the freshness of the season. Here are some quick and easy tips to help you create a warm, welcoming atmosphere without taking up too much time:

- Use pumpkins and gourds in your decorating, both outside, on your porch, and inside, in the kitchen or living room.
- Add extra color to your porch decorations with pots of mums. Arrange smaller pots with pumpkins or display larger pots by your front door.
- Use smaller outdoor items in your indoor decorating: pine cones, acorns (or other nuts still in their shell), and branches of colorful fall leaves. Pine cones and acorns can be displayed in a bowl. And branches of leaves can be arranged in a large vase. You can also add in sunflowers for extra color.
- Fill a large bowl with fall fruit, like apples and pears, to display in your kitchen or living room. You could also arrange different types of squash in a large bowl for a nice table display.
- Drape throws over the backs or arms of couches or large comfy chairs so they're ready to snuggle in. And include some fall decorative pillows to make things extra comfortable.

- Light some candles, put some simmering potpourri on the stove, or use essential oils in a diffuser to scent your home with an inviting fall aroma.

Let these small accents be little reminders, cuing you to thank God for all the joys and blessings in your life. And let's not forget the importance of taking time to rest in Jesus, even during our busiest days. "Remain in Me, and I will remain in you . . . so that you will be filled with My joy. Yes, your joy will overflow!" (John 15:4, 11 NLT).

This Pumpkin Coffee Cake recipe was chosen with the idea of "rest" in mind. While finding moments to physically rest can be tough, the irresistible taste of this coffee cake will make you want to pause and forget everything else as you savor each delightful bite. It has a delicious streusel topping and goes so well with a cup of coffee or tea.

Lord, we thank You for all the goodness You fill our lives with. Because of You, our joy is abundant and overflowing. Even in difficult times, we still have hope, peace, and joy that come from You. We know that You are always there for us, watching over us, and because of that we can have joy in any season or situation in our lives. We find joy in all the ways You bless us and provide for us each day. It's such a comfort knowing You are always thinking of us and know about everything we are going through. We thank You for the gift of each day that You give us. Help us never to take any day of our lives for granted. Teach us and guide us, day by day, and give us wisdom and strength. We love You and praise You, Father, for Your goodness and love. Amen.

pumpkin coffee cake

Enjoy this delicious coffee cake with streusel topping for breakfast, brunch, or dessert!

PREP: 20 MIN. | COOK: 35–40 MIN. | TOTAL TIME: 60 MIN. | SERVINGS: 9

STREUSEL TOPPING:

¾ cup light brown sugar, packed

⅔ cup all-purpose flour

½ teaspoon cinnamon

¼ cup butter, chilled and cut into small chunks

COFFEE CAKE:

1¾ cups all-purpose flour

1 teaspoon baking powder

½ teaspoon baking soda

½ teaspoon salt

1 teaspoon ground cinnamon

½ teaspoon ground ginger

⅓ cup canola oil

2 large eggs

¾ cup light brown sugar, packed

1 cup pumpkin puree

1. Preheat oven to 350°F. Grease or spray an 8 x 8-inch baking pan, or line with parchment paper; set aside.

2. Make the streusel topping: In a medium-size bowl, blend the brown sugar, flour, and cinnamon together, then cut in the cold butter with a pastry blender or fork until mixture is crumbly. Set aside.

3. In a large bowl, whisk together the flour, baking powder, baking soda, salt, cinnamon, and ginger.

4. In a medium-size bowl, mix the oil, eggs, brown sugar, and pumpkin puree, blending everything well.

5. Add the wet ingredients to the dry flour mixture, stirring until just combined. Spread batter into prepared pan.

6. Sprinkle streusel topping evenly over the batter, then bake for 35 to 40 minutes, until toothpick inserted in center comes out clean or almost clean. Let cake cool for at least 10 to 15 minutes, or cool completely, then cut into squares and serve.

lifelong learning

Teach me to do Your will, for You are my God.
PSALM 143:10 NLT

When back-to-school time comes around, we know fall is near! The start of a new school year is an exciting time for the students in our families, whether they're in kindergarten or high school. There are school supplies to purchase, new clothes to shop for, and the anticipation of meeting new classmates and reuniting with friends from last year. There's also the discovery and joy of learning new things. But learning doesn't stop when we graduate; it never really stops throughout our lifetime. It's a lifelong experience, and that's true even in our spiritual growth. We will never stop learning our entire lives. Jesus taught His disciples important lessons every day in the years they walked with Him. The Bible says that if we are teachable and humble, we'll be good learners. Proverbs 10:17 (THE VOICE) says, "Those who accept instruction are travelers on the road to a meaningful life." We all have seasons when we get off track. But that's how we learn and grow. God uses those situations to lovingly teach us and get us back on the right path. To be teachable means knowing we don't have all the answers and we're willing to learn what God teaches us in His Word—and to change our ways so we're aligned with His ways. It's not easy, and it's a lifelong process. But no matter our age, we can always be teachable and continue to learn to be more like Jesus.

Is there an area of your life where you could use wisdom today? Are you seeking guidance in a certain situation? Where do you need clarity and understanding? You are sure to find answers, my friend, by:

(1) Spending time in the Word.

"The LORD grants wisdom! . . . He grants a treasure of common sense to the honest. . . . You will understand what is right, just, and fair. . . . For wisdom will enter your heart, and knowledge will fill you with joy" (Proverbs 2:6–7, 9–10 NLT).

(2) Asking God.

"If any of you lacks wisdom, you should ask God, who gives generously to all without finding fault, and it will be given to you" (James 1:5 NIV).

(3) Spending time with other believers.

"The community continually committed themselves to learning what the apostles taught them" (Acts 2:42 THE VOICE).

Whatever it is that you are seeking wisdom for today, you can rest in knowing that God has gone before you (Deuteronomy 31:8 NIV). He has the answers, and if you seek His wisdom, you will find it. So while you may not have all the answers yet, He does.

Here's a good exercise for today: As you are mixing and pouring and baking the Apple Baked Oatmeal, take some time to think about all the times God has shared His wisdom with you in the past. We can all be thankful that He's such a gentle, loving, and patient Teacher!

All Scripture is inspired by God and is useful to teach us what is true. . . . It corrects us when we are wrong and teaches us to do what is right.
II TIMOTHY 3:17 NLT

Commit yourself to instruction; listen carefully to words of knowledge.
PROVERBS 23:12 NLT

Being a Christian . . . is a daily process whereby you grow to be more and more like Christ.
BILLY GRAHAM

Teach me knowledge and good judgment, for I trust Your commands.
PSALM 119:66 NIV

If you need wisdom, ask our generous God, and He will give it to you.
JAMES 1:5 NLT

Take good counsel and accept correction—that's the way to live wisely and well.
PROVERBS 19:20 THE MESSAGE

apple baked oatmeal

If you want to add some extra sweetness to this oatmeal, drizzle some maple or apple syrup or honey on top.

PREP: 10 MIN. | COOK: 35 MIN. | TOTAL TIME: 45 MIN. | SERVINGS: 8

2 cups old-fashioned rolled oats

½ cup brown sugar, packed

1½ teaspoons ground cinnamon

1 teaspoon baking powder

1/4 teaspoon salt

1½ cups milk

½ cup applesauce

2 large eggs

1½ tablespoons canola oil

2 cups diced apples (about 1½ medium-size apples), peeled or unpeeled

1. Preheat oven to 350°F. Lightly grease a 9-inch round deep dish pie plate or an 8 x 8-inch square baking pan; set aside.

2. In a large bowl, mix together the oats, brown sugar, cinnamon, baking powder, and salt.

3. In a medium-size bowl, mix the milk, applesauce, and eggs together. Pour this mixture over the dry ingredients in the large bowl and then add the oil; mix everything together well. Then stir the diced apples into the mixture.

4. Pour the oatmeal mixture into the prepared pan and bake for 35 minutes, or until set in the center. Let cool 5 to 10 minutes, then spoon or cut into slices and serve in bowls. You can pour some milk over the top of each serving if desired.

harvesttime

**God revealed Himself by doing good to you—
giving you rain for your crops and fruitful harvests season after season,
filling your stomachs with food and your hearts with joy.**

ACTS 14:17 THE VOICE

The harvest season is a time of anticipation. Farmers gather their crops in hopes of a good yield, reaping the growth of all the planting done in earlier seasons. And for gardeners, it's a time for gathering the overflow of fruits and vegetables from what was planted. Reaping happens every fall at harvesttime. We even see it in nature as squirrels and other animals scurry around, collecting nuts and seeds to store in the ground for the colder months ahead. This time of harvest shows us how God always supplies us with what we need. It's a rhythm that happens every year, and it's part of God's design, plan, and purpose for the fall season. "As long as the world exists, there will be a time for planting and a time for harvest. There will always be cold and heat, summer and winter, day and night" (Genesis 8:22 GNT). Every year, we know a time of harvest will come—just as we know there will be the cold of winter and the heat of summer. We can count on the supply of the harvest because God is always faithful to bring it. This rhythm in nature is as unchanging as God and His love for us.

Just as the harvest teaches us about God's faithfulness, we can also learn about God's perfect timing from the farmer. James 5:7 (TLB) says, "Be patient, like a farmer who waits until the autumn for his precious harvest to ripen." When a farmer cares for his fields of crops, he patiently waits as they grow, trusting that they will ripen for harvest at the right time. In a similar way, we need to patiently wait on the God who cares for us, trusting that as we wait on Him to work in our lives, He will give us a "harvest" of answered prayer at exactly the right time. It's important for us to be *patient* in waiting on God and to trust in His timing and wisdom as He guides and directs us. Only He can see the big picture, and He sees things we cannot see. He wants to bless our lives with abundance and fill our hearts with joy. He wants the very best for us. If He doesn't answer a prayer in the way we hope, it's because He is answering it in a better way. Sometimes it may seem like God is delaying answering our prayers, but we can trust that He always give us what we need when we need it. His timing is not our timing—it's so much better!

As you enjoy this harvest season, maybe you'll have some time to make Pumpkin-Pecan Bread. The fall season just isn't the same without it! Think about the abundant ways God has blessed you this season as you mix the pumpkin puree, cinnamon, and other good things into the batter. And thank Him in advance for how He is working to fill the needs you are praying about right now. You can rest in His promise in Philippians 4:19 that He will provide all you need.

Lord, You are a God of abundance, and we are so grateful for how You provide for us in every way. Your supply of love, care, and provision never run out. You even know what we need before we ask and are always so faithful to watch over us, guide us, and protect us. We thank You for the beauty and the bounty of the harvest season and the lessons You teach us from it. Give us the patience and trust we need to stay strong in our faith as we wait on You to work out Your good plans in our lives. Remind us that Your ways are always best for us. And Father, let us find peace and rest in knowing that we can give all our needs and cares to You, and You will provide for us in Your perfect timing, exactly when we need it. We love You and are so grateful for Your amazing love for us. Amen.

pumpkin pecan bread

Fall just isn't fall without pumpkin bread!

PREP: 15 MIN. | COOK: 60–70 MIN. | TOTAL TIME: 1 HR. 25 MIN. | SERVINGS: 10

3½ cups all-purpose flour

2 teaspoons baking soda

1½ teaspoons salt

1 teaspoon baking powder

2 teaspoons ground cinnamon

2 teaspoons ground nutmeg

3 cups granulated sugar

⅔ cup milk

1 cup canola oil

5 large eggs, beaten

1 (15-ounce) can pumpkin puree (not pie filling)

1½ cups chopped pecans

1. Preheat oven to 350°F. Grease or spray two 9 x 5-inch loaf pans; set aside.
2. In a large bowl, mix together the flour, baking soda, salt, baking powder, cinnamon, nutmeg, and sugar.
3. Add the milk and canola oil to the dry ingredients, mixing everything together.
4. Stir in the eggs and then the pumpkin, mixing everything well.
5. Fold in the pecans, stirring until evenly incorporated into the batter.
6. Divide the batter equally between the greased loaf pans and bake for 60 to 70 minutes, or until a toothpick in the center comes out clean. Let loaves cool in pans for 15 to 20 minutes, then remove to a wire rack to cool completely.

your cheering section

**With God on our side like this,
how can we lose?**

ROMANS 8:31 THE MESSAGE

With football season here, many of us are cheering on our favorite teams. If you have kids who play sports, you know how much you love cheering for them! Parents cheer faithfully for their children, in everything from football games to school projects to church events. "You can do it!" and "Keep going!" we say. Parents are the most loyal fans. God, our heavenly Father, is like that—He's our biggest fan. He cheers us on every day as we journey through life. He cheers us on as we're winning and cheers us on when we stumble and make mistakes. God never stops cheering for us; He is always *for* us, supporting us and loving us. Psalm 56:9 (TLB) says, "This one thing I know: God is for me!" He watches over us and gives us the strength we need each day: "The eyes of the Lord search the whole earth in order to strengthen those whose hearts are fully committed to Him" (II Chronicles 16:9 NLT).

We have others cheering us on from heaven too: the great cloud of witnesses that Hebrews 12:1 (NIV) tells us about: "Since we are surrounded by such a great cloud of witnesses, let us throw off everything that hinders and the sin that so easily entangles. And let us run with perseverance the race marked out for us." This great cloud of witnesses can also be described as "those who have gone before," all the people of faith who are in heaven now, like those in our families who have gone on to heaven—parents, grandparents, aunts, uncles . . . those who have left us a legacy of faith. And our heroes of the faith that we read about in the Bible—Noah, Abraham, Sarah, Moses, and others—they're an inspiration to us, having persevered their whole lives as they lived in faith (see Hebrews 11). These saints in heaven are all cheering us on.

So if you ever feel as if you're alone in this race, or if the struggles you're facing are too much, find comfort in the fact that while God will never leave your side, you also have a cloud of witnesses who overcame many obstacles of their own, and they are cheering your name.

Side note: On game day, if you're watching a game from home or tailgating, you could make this Loaded Baked-Potato Dip to snack on. It's loaded with lots of good things: sour cream, cheddar cheese, bacon, and more.

I keep working toward that day
when I will finally be all that Christ
saved me for and wants me to be.
PHILIPPIANS 3:12 TLB

Let us press on to know Him.
HOSEA 6:3 NLT

This I know: God is on my side!
PSALM 56:9 NLT

God loves each of us
as if there were only one of us.
SAINT AUGUSTINE

The moment we get tired in the waiting,
God's Spirit is right alongside helping us along.
ROMANS 8:26 THE MESSAGE

The prophets . . . through faith
conquered kingdoms, administered justice,
and gained what was promised.
HEBREWS 11:32–33 NIV

loaded baked potato dip

Serve this dip with wavy potato chips, waffle fries, or pretzels.

PREP: 10 MIN. | COOK: 0 MIN. | TOTAL TIME: 10 MIN. | SERVINGS: 8

- 2 cups (16 ounces) sour cream or light sour cream
- 1 (1-ounce) package ranch dressing and seasoning mix
- 2 cups (8 ounces) shredded sharp cheddar cheese, divided
- ⅓ cup green onions, thinly sliced
- ½ cup real bacon pieces or bits (from a 2.5-ounce package)
- Optional: salt and pepper to taste and/or a dash of hot sauce
- For garnish: remaining ¼ cup cheddar cheese, ½ to 1 tablespoon each green onion slices, and real bacon pieces or bits

1. In a large bowl, mix the sour cream and ranch dressing mix, blending well.
2. Stir in 1¾ cups of the shredded cheddar cheese, the sliced green onions, and the bacon pieces or bits. If desired, add some salt and pepper to taste, or a dash of hot sauce.
3. Spoon dip into a serving bowl, then cover and refrigerate for an hour before serving (can also be refrigerated overnight).
4. Before serving, garnish with remaining ¼ cup cheddar cheese and ½ to 1 tablespoon each green onion slices and real bacon pieces or bits.

grateful always

**Always be joyful. Never stop praying.
Be thankful in all circumstances,
for this is God's will for you who belong to Christ Jesus.**
1 THESSALONIANS 5:16–18 NLT

In this season when we celebrate Thanksgiving, we reflect on all that we're grateful for. It's a time of celebration, as we take time to pause, enjoy a holiday meal, and give thanks to God. And we have so much to be thankful for—look around you at this very moment and count three things you're thankful for. Maybe it's the house you're in, the people you are around, the free magnetic calendar you got in the mail today. Too often we wait to show our gratitude to God only when big life changes happen, but there is so much to be thankful for in this very moment.

And what about the challenging times? Do we have a heart full of gratitude in the hard times? First Thessalonians 5:18 (NLT) tells us, "Be thankful in all circumstances." This Scripture is saying we can be thankful not just in times of blessing, but also in times of difficulty. That sounds hard to do, but when you think about it, we can be grateful in our ever-changing circumstances because God is the Source of our provision and blessings, and He *never* changes. Whether we find ourselves in good times, busy times, or hard times, we know our unchanging God is still taking care of us: "I, God, will never forget you" (Isaiah 49:15 THE VOICE). We may not understand how He is working on our behalf during the tough times, but we can always be thankful, because He is always faithful.

Having a grateful heart in all circumstances doesn't come to us naturally; it takes some changes in our mindset to grow in gratitude and think grateful thoughts. We can start in our prayer time, giving thanks to God for the blessings He gives us each day: the house we live in . . . the car we drive . . . the job that provides for our family . . . the food He blesses us with at our meals . . . the beautiful sunsets we see every evening . . . nothing is too big or too small to give Him thanks for. Growing in gratitude is also a matter of shifting our focus—from the difficulties we're facing, or from what we don't have, to knowing God is with us in our difficulties, recognizing all that we *do* have through Him.

Gratitude will grow more and more within us as we "come before Him with thanksgiving" every day (Psalm 95:2 NIV). Think of each morning as a new opportunity to thank God for all He does. It's a sweet way to start your day.

Speaking of sweet . . . here's a sweet and easy snack recipe you can try for a fall get-together: Caramel-Apple Dip. It makes a great snack for your family, a group gathering, or even game day. As you melt the caramel with the other creamy ingredients in a saucepan, take some time to think grateful thoughts about your day and consider what you can thank God for!

Lord, we come to You with grateful hearts for all the ways You bless us and fill our lives with so many good things. Because of Your abundant and unconditional love, we can live joyfully and thankfully every day of our lives, no matter what our circumstances are. We can be grateful in every season, whether we're experiencing good days or difficult ones, because we know we are in Your care and You give us so much to be thankful for. Help us to remember to focus on You instead of any challenging circumstances we may face, knowing You will work through those for our good. We thank You that You always hold us close to Your heart and that You promise never to forget us. You are always so faithful. Help us to see Your blessings all around us as we go through each day and never take any of them for granted. Our hearts are filled with love for You and gratefulness to You for Your goodness to us. Amen.

caramel apple dip

*This recipe makes about two and a half cups of dip.
You can heat up any leftover dip and use it as an ice cream topping.*

PREP: 25 MIN. | COOK: 5–7 MIN. | TOTAL TIME: 25 MIN. | SERVINGS: 8

- 1 (11-ounce) bag caramels, unwrapped, or Kraft Caramel Bits
- 1 (14-ounce) can sweetened condensed milk
- ½ cup (1 stick) unsalted butter
- Optional garnish: 2 teaspoons chopped peanuts (or pecans) or toffee bits, or 1 teaspoon each of nuts and toffee bits
- Sliced apples to serve with the dip

1. Add the caramels, sweetened condensed milk, and butter to a small- to medium-size saucepan saucepan and cook over medium-low heat, stirring frequently until mixture is smooth, creamy, and well-blended.

2. Pour the caramel dip into a small bowl. If desired, garnish the top of the dip with a sprinkle of chopped nuts and/or toffee bits.

3. Serve the dip while still warm with sliced apples. You could also serve with other fruit such as sliced pears, sliced bananas, or pineapple chunks, or with pretzels.

4. Refrigerate any leftover dip for up to 2 weeks.

gathering together

*"Where two or three gather in my name,
there am I with them."*

MATTHEW 18:20 NIV

Fall gatherings are one of the best things about this season! It could be a small group or a large one, but the size of the gathering doesn't matter—it's who we are gathering with that's important. We might gather with friends outside for an evening bonfire and enjoy hot cocoa and s'mores. Or with neighbors to watch a football game and snack on our favorite dips. And then there's gathering for meals. It could be a small, simple meal with a friend or a large dinner with lots of family. Gathering is a special time when we enjoy being together and catching up with each other, savoring moments of great conversation, laughter, and good food. These times of fellowship remind us how important it is to stay connected with each other. We need time for bonding, supporting, and encouraging each other. We're not meant to do life on our own!

We can find a good example of "doing life together" from what Paul tells us about the early Christians in the book of Acts. Not only did they come together as a group to learn from the teaching of the apostles, they also gathered together "for fellowship, breaking bread, and praying. . . . They were unified as they worshiped at the temple day after day. In homes, they broke bread and shared meals with glad and generous hearts" (Acts 2:42, 46 THE VOICE). The believers in the early church spent a lot of time together—growing in their faith, gathering for meals and fellowship, praying, and worshiping together. They were able to encourage and motivate each other, help each other, and be like family to each other. As they grew closer to the Lord, they grew closer to one another.

The connection and community we have is a special bond. Even Jesus had community with the disciples, with His friend Lazarus, and with others who were close to Him. God wants us to encourage, care for, and be there for one another—that's what true community is all about. As we grow together, we can make each other better: "Let us consider how to inspire each other to greater love and to righteous deeds, not forgetting to gather as a community . . . but encouraging each other" (Hebrews 10:24–25 THE VOICE).

As you grow in community with other believers, having a meal together is a wonderful way to get to know each other better. Whether you're hosting a meal or bringing something for a potluck, this Apple-Pear Salad makes a wonderful addition to any meal. It's filled with lots of great fall flavors: chopped or sliced apples and pears, dried cranberries, and more. As you toss all these ingredients together, think about your own community and the ways your group has grown closer together. If you don't have a community group, ask God to lead you to the one that's best for you.

Encourage each other and build each other up, just as you are already doing.
I THESSALONIANS 5:11 NLT

Two people are better off than one, for they can help each other succeed. If one person falls, the other can reach out and help.
ECCLESIASTES 4:9-10 NLT

To gather with God's people in united adoration of the Father is as necessary to the Christian life as prayer.
MARTIN LUTHER

Warmly welcome each other into the church, just as Christ has warmly welcomed you.
ROMANS 15:7 TLB

When we come together something beautiful will happen as we are encouraged by each other's faith.
ROMANS 1:12 THE VOICE

All the believers met together constantly and shared everything with each other.
ACTS 2:44 TLB

apple-pear salad

You can substitute your favorite vinaigrette for the oil and vinegar in this recipe.

PREP: 25 MIN. | COOK: 0 MIN. | TOTAL TIME: 25 MIN. | SERVINGS: 8

8 to 10 cups mixed salad greens

½ cup red onion, chopped

2 medium-size apples, chopped or sliced

2 medium-size pears, chopped or sliced

1 cup dried cranberries

1 cup shaved or shredded Parmesan cheese

¾ cup sliced almonds

3 tablespoons olive oil (or your favorite salad oil)

1½ tablespoons apple cider vinegar (or your favorite vinegar)

Salt and pepper to taste

1. In a large bowl, add the mixed greens, red onion, apples and pears, dried cranberries, Parmesan cheese, and sliced almonds.

2. Drizzle the olive oil over the salad ingredients, then the vinegar. Season with salt and pepper.

3. Toss the salad ingredients well, until everything is coated.

4. Garnish with additional cheese, cranberries, and almonds, if desired, and serve.

NOTE: If you're using oil and vinegar for the salad but would like a sweeter taste, drizzle 1 tablespoon honey over the salad ingredients when you add the oil, vinegar, salt, and pepper, and toss well.

the right path

The Lord says, "I will guide you along the best pathway for your life. I will advise you and watch over you."
PSALM 32:8 NLT

Many of us enjoy taking walks or hikes in the fall to enjoy the colorful foliage. When hiking, there are several paths to choose from. Some paths are longer than others, some are steeper and more difficult to navigate, and some may offer more striking views along the way. Choosing just the right path isn't always easy.

The pathways of our lives can be similar to the ones we hike on. As we journey through life, many paths unfold before us, and we're faced with lots of decisions to make. Which path to take? Which way to turn? It might involve moving to another state, buying a home, or deciding on a job offer. How can we know what path is best for us? It can be overwhelming at times. But when we look to God for wisdom in the choices we need to make, we can be confident He will show us the right path. He promises to guide us, and He tells us He will advise us and watch over us.

God knows every detail of our days and lives and knows what's best for us. "You saw me before I was born and scheduled each day of my life before I began to breathe. Every day was recorded in Your book!" (Psalm 139:16 TLB). He knows us better than we know ourselves, and He knows what we need before we even ask Him (see Matthew 6:8). Because He is all-knowing and only He can see what's ahead, we can completely trust Him to show us the best path to move forward on.

There will be times God clearly calls us to take a path that will take us out of our comfort zone. We may be a little fearful stepping out onto this new path. At times like this, let's remember what Proverbs 3:5–6 (NLT) tells us, "Trust in the Lord with all your heart; do not depend on your own understanding. Seek His will in all you do, and He will show you which path to take." Our understanding is limited, but God's is *unlimited*, and He has a purpose for each path He calls us to walk on. He will always equip us with what we need for our journey. We can always move forward with confidence, knowing He is guiding us, watching over us, and teaching us every step of the way. Isn't it comforting to know that whatever path you're on, God is always with you? He goes before you, making the rough places in your journey smooth (Isaiah 45:2).

As if that wasn't comforting enough, why not top it off with the cozy, delicious warmth of Corn Casserole? It's definitely comfort food and so easy to make!

Lord, we're so blessed to have a loving Father who guides us and watches over us. It comforts us to know that we can always look to You, knowing You will show us the right path to take and that it will be the best choice for us. It's amazing to think how well You know us. You know about every single detail of our days. You know about every need we have, and You care about all of our worries and fears. We thank You that we can release these burdens to You so we can move ahead lightly and freely. Even when things look uncertain or uncomfortable to us, You calm us with Your peace, and Your Word reminds us that You are always in control. Help us grow in our trust in You, remembering that You always know what's best for us and You go before us, smoothing out the rough places in our paths. We praise You and thank You for guiding us every step of the way in the beautiful journey You have planned for us. Amen.

corn casserole

This casserole makes a great side dish for the holidays!

PREP: 10 MIN. | COOK: 45-50 MIN. | TOTAL TIME: 60 MIN. | SERVINGS: 6-9

- 1 (15-ounce) can whole-kernel corn, drained
- 1 (14.75-ounce) can cream-style corn
- 1 (8.5-ounce) box corn muffin mix
- ½ cup (1 stick) butter, melted
- 1 cup (8 ounces) sour cream or plain Greek yogurt
- 3 large eggs, lightly beaten

1. Preheat oven to 350°F. Lightly grease an 8 x 8-inch or 9 x 9-inch baking pan or casserole dish with butter or cooking spray; set aside.
2. In a large bowl, combine the corn and cream-style corn with the corn muffin mix, then add the melted butter and sour cream or Greek yogurt. Add the eggs, mixing everything well. Pour into prepared baking pan.
3. Bake for 45 to 50 minutes, or until casserole is set and middle is firm.
4. Remove from oven and serve while hot or warm.

bountiful blessings

**You crown the year with a bountiful harvest;
even the hard pathways overflow with abundance.**

PSALM 65:11 NLT

When we hear the word *bountiful*, we may think of bushel baskets overflowing with red and golden apples, a field filled with tall and radiant sunflowers, or an endless patch of pumpkins of all shapes and sizes. This abundance is amazing when we see it with our own eyes. There's so much goodness and beauty, it's hard to take it all in! God blesses us so bountifully through His creation.

Bountiful can also be defined as generous, lavish, and even extravagant. Many of these words are used in Scripture to describe how God loves us, cares for us, and blesses us. "You lavish Your favor on all creatures" (Psalm 145:16 THE MESSAGE). He is described as "this most patient God, extravagant in love" (Joel 2:13 THE MESSAGE). The depth of His love for us is hard to fully comprehend. Ephesians 3:18 (TLB) talks about "how long, how wide, how deep, and how high" His love is for us, and verse 19 adds that His love is "so great that you will never see the end of it or fully know or understand it." What a blessing it is to know that we are loved so fully, completely, unconditionally, and *extravagantly* by God!

His extravagant love and care for us are also evident in some of the miracles Jesus performed. Like when He had come across some discouraged fishermen with two boats who had worked all night and hadn't caught any fish. Jesus told one of them, Simon, to let the nets down again from his boat. Simon did, and much to his surprise, "They caught such a large number of fish that their nets began to break. So they signaled their partners in the other boat to come and help them, and they came and filled both boats so full that they began to sink" (Luke 5:6–7 NIV). Jesus didn't just meet the needs of the fishermen; He provided for them *extravagantly*! So much that the nets started to break and the boats started to sink. In II Corinthians 9:8 (THE VOICE) we're told, "God is ready to overwhelm you with more blessings than you could ever imagine so that you'll always be taken care of in every way and you'll have more than enough to share." God is a God of *more than enough*. He loves to bless us bountifully and extravagantly, and He promises to take care of us in every way.

This doesn't just apply to material things. God's love, peace, and joy flow into every area of our lives, ensuring that we are taken care of in every way—physically, emotionally, and spiritually. So whatever you are facing today, take heart. We serve a God who loves us so deeply and extravagantly, and He is always ready to meet our needs—more than enough, every time.

As you go about preparing today's recipe, contemplate the depth of God's extravagant love for you.

*You can be sure that God will
take care of everything you need.*
PHILIPPIANS 4:19 THE MESSAGE

It is only with gratitude that life becomes rich.
DIETRICH BONHOEFFER

*I will praise You, L*ORD*, with all my heart;
I will tell of all the wonderful things You have done.*
PSALM 9:1 GNT

*He has showered down upon us the richness of His grace—
for how well He understands us and knows
what is best for us at all times.*
EPHESIANS 1:7-8 TLB

God's unfailing love and faithfulness came through Jesus Christ.
JOHN 1:17 NLT

*Your faithful love is higher than the heavens,
and Your faithfulness reaches to the clouds.*
PSALM 108:4 CSB

secret ingredient chili

*The secret ingredient is unsweetened cocoa powder.
It gives the chili a rich flavor!*

PREP: 20 MIN. | COOK: 60 MIN. | TOTAL TIME: 1 HR. 20 MIN. | SERVINGS: 6

1½ pounds ground beef

1 large onion, chopped

2 (15-ounce) cans red kidney beans, rinsed and drained

1 (15-ounce) can black beans, rinsed and drained

1 (28-ounce) can diced tomatoes, undrained

1 (15-ounce) can tomato sauce

3 tablespoons chili powder

½ tablespoon ground cumin

1 tablespoon unsweetened cocoa powder

2 cloves minced garlic

Salt and pepper to taste

Optional toppings for chili: sour cream, shredded cheddar cheese, and chopped green onions

1. In a large saucepan, cook the ground beef and chopped onion over medium heat until the beef is no longer pink; drain the fat.

2. Add the beans, diced tomatoes, tomato sauce, chili powder, cumin, unsweetened cocoa powder, minced garlic, and salt and pepper, if desired.

3. Reduce heat and simmer, covered, for 1 hour, stirring occasionally.

4. Top the chili with any or all of the following: sour cream, shredded cheddar cheese, and chopped green onions.

NOTE: For a spicier chili, use a 28-ounce can of diced tomatoes with green chilies instead of regular diced tomatoes.

traditions and remembering

**I remember the days gone by;
I think about all that You have done.**
PSALM 143:5 GNT

Each holiday season, we look forward to family traditions. They bring back sweet memories, and there's something comforting about these familiar ways of doing things. At Thanksgiving, we enjoy a nice meal with family and friends—feasting on the traditional turkey, dressing, sweet potatoes, and pumpkin pie. Some of us have large gatherings and others have smaller ones. Many of us start our meal thanking God for His goodness, and others share what they're grateful for around the table. Some of our Thanksgiving family traditions are similar and some are unique, but the ones that remind us of why we come together are the most important: to give thanks to God for His abundant blessings and to remember His faithfulness.

Scripture shows us the importance of remembering how God has worked in our lives. Psalm 77:11–12 (NIV) says, "I will remember the deeds of the Lord; yes, I will remember Your miracles of long ago. I will consider all Your works and meditate on all Your mighty deeds." Our faith is strengthened when we remember the amazing things God has done for us. We need to remember and share these things with others; it's part of our story and our legacy. Moses told the Israelites when they were close to the promised land, "Be careful never to forget what you yourself have seen. Do not let these memories escape from your mind as long as you live! And be sure to pass them on to your children and grandchildren" (Deuteronomy 4:9 NLT).

The more we remember the life-changing ways God has worked in our past, the stronger our faith grows in how He is working in our lives today. Remembering what He has already done assures us that He is always working for our good in every situation we face and that nothing is too difficult for Him to accomplish. He can work through any challenges that come our way. That gives us confidence for the future, too, knowing that He will always take care of us and do what's best for us.

We can start our own tradition of remembering God's faithfulness every day by reflecting on how we see Him work as He answers prayers, makes a way through our wilderness season, or provides what we need at just the right moment. Let's thank Him in our prayer time, write a note in our journal about it, worship Him with songs, and share about His goodness in our lives with others.

Here's another tradition to keep in mind for fall—a sweet and tasty one! Bake up some Chocolate-Chip-Coconut-Oatmeal Cookies. Oatmeal cookies are a wonderful treat for this time of year, and these particular ones are chewy and full of good things. The kids can enjoy them with milk, and you can enjoy them with a cup of hot coffee or tea on chilly day. While you stir the cookie dough and place it on your baking sheets, take some time to remember how God has worked in your life recently. And thank Him for how He is working now.

Lord, You fill our lives with an abundance of good things. You are so faithful to take care of us. Help us to always remember and never take for granted all that You have done for us. We thank You for the joy and comfort of traditions that remind us of Your blessings and faithfulness. They help us remember all You have done for us and all You continue to do. May we never forget Your goodness to us in every way, and may we be faithful in sharing about that with others. You are our gracious and loving Father, continually supplying all our needs each day. Let us always remember that Your faithfulness surrounds us, no matter what we go through. Thank You for all the ways You have worked in our lives and how You are actively working right now. We love You and are so grateful to You for Your overflowing and never-ending goodness in our lives. Amen.

chocolate chip coconut oatmeal cookies

Coconut flakes add some extra sweetness to this oatmeal cookie.

PREP: 20 MIN. | COOK: 15 MIN. | TOTAL TIME: 35 MIN. | SERVINGS: 27

1 cup coconut oil

1 cup granulated sugar

1 cup light brown sugar, packed

2 large eggs

1 teaspoon vanilla extract

2 tablespoons milk

1½ cups all-purpose unbleached flour

½ teaspoon salt

1 teaspoon baking soda

3 cups quick-cooking oats

1 cup sweetened coconut flakes

1 cup semisweet chocolate chips

1. Preheat oven to 350°F. Line cookie sheets with parchment paper; set aside.

2. In a large bowl, blend coconut oil and sugars. Add the eggs, vanilla extract, and milk, blending everything together well. Then add the flour, salt, and baking soda, mixing well.

3. Stir in the oats, coconut flakes, and chocolate chips, distributing them evenly in batter.

4. Drop by ¼ cup-fuls onto prepared cookie sheets, about 2 inches apart. (You can also use a scoop to drop the cookie dough on the sheet.)

5. Bake for 15 minutes or until golden brown and centers are set. Let cool for a few minutes on pan, then transfer to wired rack to cool completely.

embrace each season

**For everything that happens in life—
there is a season, a right time for everything under heaven.**
ECCLESIASTES 3:1 THE VOICE

We all have a favorite season. Some of us love the colorful beauty and brisk air of fall best, and others are more drawn to the warmer days and blooming flowers that springtime brings. But when we embrace how God is working in each season of our lives—whether it be a difficult season, restful season, or waiting season—we can see God's goodness. God never wastes any experience we go through. Just as He has a purpose for every season in nature, He has a purpose for every season in our lives. And He uses each phase and stage to grow us, teach us, and bless us.

If you picked up this book, then you are probably in a busy season—one in which every minute of every day is packed with tasks, responsibilities, and commitments. Did you know you could take your weariness to Jesus? Matthew 11:28 (NIV) says, "Come to Me, all you who are weary and burdened, and I will give you rest." Jesus promises rest—not just physical rest, but rest for our souls. He may not take away the tasks on your to-do list, but He will give you peace of mind as you go about your days. You see, sometimes we tend to think that if we just push through, everything will eventually calm down. But God offers us a better way. Rest doesn't always mean stopping everything—it's about learning to rest in Him even while we keep moving. The next time you find yourself feeling stressed and overwhelmed, talk to God. Ask Him what your next steps should be. Ask Him to slow your racing thoughts, and to replace the whirlwind in your head with clarity. Release it all into God's capable hands.

Isaiah 40:29-31 (NIV) says "He gives strength to the weary and increases the power of the weak. Even youths grow tired and weary, and young men stumble and fall; but those who hope in the Lord will renew their strength. They will soar on wings like eagles; they will run and not grow weary, they will walk and not be faint." In this verse, we find that sometimes God's answer to our chaotic lives is to increase our power so we can keep going, to renew our spirits so that we are ready to face the day, to give us wings like eagles so we soar higher than ever before. So while your to-do list may only grow, and your daily demands may only increase over the next few months, you can take comfort in the fact that God promises to equip you with all the strength you need to accomplish His will for your life.

Today's recipe for Mini–Apple Bundt Cakes is a delicious treat that's perfect for any fall event. Even on busy days, this simple recipe offers both a quick break and a sweet reward without adding stress to your schedule.

How great is Your goodness . . . . You have stored up great blessings for those who trust and reverence You.
PSALM 31:19 TLB

We walk by faith, not by sight.
II CORINTHIANS 5:7 CSB

The more impossible the situation, the greater God accomplishes His work.
CHARLES R. SWINDOLL

Take your everyday, ordinary life—your sleeping, eating, going-to-work, and walking-around life—and place it before God as an offering. Embracing what God does for you is the best thing you can do for Him.
ROMANS 12:1 THE MESSAGE

Don't be afraid of change, because it is leading you to a new beginning.
JOYCE MEYER

Let us keep our eyes fixed on Jesus, on whom our faith depends from beginning to end.
HEBREWS 12:2 GNT

mini apple bundt cakes

You can substitute spice cake mix for the yellow cake mix in this recipe.

PREP: 15 MIN. | COOK: 18–22 MIN. | TOTAL TIME: 37 MIN. | SERVINGS: 12

- 1 (15.25-ounce) box yellow cake mix
- ½ cup apple juice
- ½ cup water
- 3 large eggs
- ⅓ cup cinnamon applesauce
- 2 teaspoons ground cinnamon
- 1 teaspoon pure vanilla extract
- 2 cups apples, diced
- Powdered sugar for dusting

1. Preheat oven to 350°F. Grease two 6-cake mini Bundt pans (or jumbo muffin pans); set aside.

2. In a large bowl, add dry cake mix, apple juice, water, and eggs, mixing everything well. Stir in the applesauce, cinnamon, and vanilla, mixing until blended, then fold in the diced apples.

3. Divide batter evenly among each mini Bundt (they'll each be about ⅔ full).

4. Bake for 18 to 22 minutes or until toothpick inserted in centers comes out clean or almost clean. Let cool in pans about 10 minutes, then invert on wire rack (you may need to loosen the edges of the Bundts with a knife if they are sticking to the pan). Cool on rack an additional 10 to 15 minutes.

5. Sprinkle the tops of each mini Bundt with powdered sugar, dusting lightly, then arrange on a platter or cake stand and serve.

THE CHANGING SEASONS:
fall-winter

When the colors of fall start to fade, we know the snowy white of winter will soon be here. We're thankful for the bountiful ways God blessed us during the harvest season and what we learned from God's creation. Like how the turning leaves on the trees showed us how change can bring beauty to our lives and the falling leaves taught us about the freedom of letting go. And how nature's pathways reminded us we can always trust God to guide us in the right direction on our journeys. Some of us cheered on our favorite football teams, and we realized we all have a cheering section in heaven, encouraging us and rooting for us. We enjoyed cozy moments in our homes and reflected on how God is so faithful in supplying our needs. We saw that it's important to embrace every season, even our busy ones, and that God has a special purpose for us in each one. And we know this will always be true: we are loved fully, unconditionally, and extravagantly by God, day after day and season after season.

And now we look ahead to winter and all the gifts this new season brings: the peaceful beauty of nature as it begins a season of rest, the anticipation of the first snowfall that never fails to fill us with wonder, and most important of all, the celebration we look forward to at Christmas as we remember the gift God gave us in Jesus. It's a busy season of decorating our homes with wreaths and garlands and twinkling lights, enjoying holiday gatherings and events, and helping others who are in need. Somehow we find time for bundling up in our warm coats and mittens to go ice-skating, build a snowman, or go for a drive and admire the holiday lights. And in the evenings, we love the relaxing coziness of sitting by a crackling fire or flickering candles as we enjoy hot cocoa and cookies with lots of sprinkles.

In the midst of all the busyness, it's good for us to slow down and remember that winter is also a season of rest. We can see this in nature, in the stillness and quiet, and rest is important in our lives too—it refreshes and restores us. Jesus tells us, "Come to Me . . . and I will give you rest" (Matthew 11:28 NIV). As we move forward into winter and all the fun and festivities it brings, let's also take time for reflection and rest. Let's quiet ourselves so we can focus on what the holiday season is really all about and all that we have through Him—love, joy, peace, hope, and everlasting life. Let's always remember that Jesus is the Light of our world and keep Him at the heart of our celebrations and seasons.

*Lord, You are the Giver of so many good things.
Our lives are filled with more blessings than we can
count, and they continue to flow from Your generous
hand. We see Your unconditional, extravagant love
for us through the ways You provide and take care
of us. We're so thankful for Your guidance and how
You're always with us, every minute of every day.
Your presence comforts us, and Your strength gets
us through the tough times. Thank You for the ways
You speak so personally to our hearts through Your
Word and Your Spirit. It reminds us that we are always
seen, heard, and loved by You. As we embrace the
winter season, let it be a time when we can find true
rest in You, undistracted by all the busyness around
us. Fill us with Your peace and joy and let this season
remind us that all good and perfect gifts come from
You, including the greatest Gift of all—Jesus. Amen.*

winter

Have you ever traveled to where snow is made? . . .
Or to the place from which the wind blows?

JOB 38:22–23 THE MESSAGE

The quiet hush of winter invites us to slow down and enjoy the peaceful calm of the season. One of the wonders of winter is waking up to see a blanket of freshly fallen snow covering fields and hills, with snow-covered trees glistening under the sun. We enjoy the fresh air of these frosty days, but we also love to snuggle in the warmth of our homes. It's the time of year for comfort food and steaming cups of coffee and tea. We love the bright tastes of winter citrus in the mornings—like the sweet and tangy clementine—as we thank God for the gift of another day, fresh and new. Later on, our kitchens are filled with the savory aromas of hearty soups and stews that we enjoy with crusty breads. And there's the comforting taste of sweet potatoes covered with marshmallows and the tartness of fresh cranberries in sauces and holiday desserts. Life-giving, good things abound in our kitchen even in the stillness of winter.

And it's in this beautiful stillness that God gets our attention: "Be still, and know that I am God" (Psalm 46:10 NIV). It's a time for us to pause, reflect, and notice the quiet, small things in our ordinary days that God can use to teach us. Let's wait expectantly for Him to speak in our times of quiet. Let's not miss a word of what He is saying—or miss anything He wants to show us. Winter is here, and this season is full of so much beauty and grace for us to discover and experience. Let's not miss a moment of it!

rest for your soul

"Come to Me, all you who are weary . . .
and I will give you rest."

MATTHEW 11:28 NIV

The holiday season brightens our days with so much fun: cookie baking, attending Christmas pageants and plays, and enjoying festive get-togethers. But it also wears us out! All the shopping, planning, gift-wrapping, and so many other things take up our time as we try to juggle tasks at home and at work. We have so much on our minds and so many details to keep track of. With everything going on, we would probably agree that *weary* is a word that truly describes how we feel. And we realize that we really need rest—we need to slow down and have moments of calm and quiet to soothe and restore our souls. We can only find this kind of deep rest through Jesus: "Come to Me, all you who are weary. . . . Take My yoke upon you and learn from Me, for I am gentle and humble in heart, and you will find rest for your souls" (Matthew 11:28–29 NIV).

Rest for our souls, or *soul rest*, is exactly the kind of rest we need—the kind that restores not only our bodies, but our minds, our hearts, and our spirits. To receive it, Jesus tells us to *come to Him and learn from Him*. We see many times in the Bible how He went away from the crowds that surrounded Him to a place of quiet—where He found rest and spent time in prayer with His Father: "After dismissing the crowds, He went up on the mountain by Himself to pray. Well into the night, He was there alone" (Matthew 14:23 CSB). And Luke 5:16 (THE MESSAGE) tells us, "As often as possible Jesus withdrew to out-of-the-way places for prayer." These times of prayer and quiet with God restored Him, and they can restore us too. Following the example of Jesus, we can experience true rest for our souls as we get away to a quiet place to spend time with God, praying, reading the Bible, meditating on Scripture, and spending time being "still" and listening to His voice.

Throughout our hectic season, let's find true, deep soul rest in Jesus. Let's take a few moments to withdraw from the busyness in our days and spend quiet time with our loving Father. He knows our needs, cares, and all the things that overwhelm us, and there's no load we carry that is too heavy for Him to lighten for us. Let's come to Him to rest in His love, be filled with His peace, and be restored by His grace.

Cranberry Quick Bread might be just what you're needing for an easy winter breakfast! As it bakes, take time to pray, relax, and soak up some rest for your soul—from the generous supply that Jesus is always ready to provide.

*It is senseless for you to work so hard
from early morning until late at night . . .
for God wants His loved ones to get their proper rest.*
PSALM 127:2 TLB

*On the seventh day God had finished His work of
creation, so He rested from all His work.*
GENESIS 2:2 NLT

*Our rest lies in looking to the Lord,
not to ourselves.*
WATCHMAN NEE

*The Lord is my shepherd, I lack nothing.
He makes me lie down in green pastures,
He leads me beside quiet waters, He refreshes my soul.*
PSALM 23:1-3 NIV

*"My Presence will go with you,
and I will give you rest."*
EXODUS 33:14 NIV

*There still remains for God's people
a rest like God's resting on the seventh day.
For those who receive that rest which God promised
will rest from their own work, just as God rested from His.*
HEBREWS 4:9-10 GNT

cranberry quick bread

You can use fresh or frozen cranberries in this loaf.

PREP: 15 MIN. | COOK: 45–50 MIN. | TOTAL TIME: 65 MIN. | SERVINGS: 10

- 1½ cups all-purpose flour
- ¾ cup granulated sugar
- 1 teaspoon baking powder
- ¼ teaspoon baking soda
- ¼ teaspoon salt
- 1½ teaspoons cinnamon
- 1 large egg
- ½ cup orange juice
- 2 tablespoons butter, melted
- 2 to 3 teaspoons orange extract
- 1½ cups fresh or frozen cranberries, coarsely chopped

1. Preheat oven to 350°F. Grease and flour an 8 x 4-inch loaf pan; set aside.
2. In a large bowl, blend flour, sugar, baking powder, baking soda, salt, and cinnamon; set aside.
3. In small bowl, mix the egg, orange juice, melted butter, and orange extract. Add to the dry ingredients in the large bowl, stirring just until moistened. Fold in the chopped cranberries and stir until evenly distributed in batter.
4. Pour batter into the prepared loaf pan and bake for 45 to 50 minutes, until toothpick inserted in center comes out clean.
5. Cool in pan for 5 to 10 minutes, then remove loaf from pan and cool completely on a wire rack. Then slice and serve. You can also serve slices spread with softened butter or cream cheese.

good gifts

**Every good gift and every perfect present
comes from heaven;
it comes down from God,
the Creator of the heavenly lights.**
JAMES 1:17 GNT

Christmastime is often called "the season of giving." We think about gift ideas for family and friends as we get ready to do our holiday shopping. Whether we have a short or long shopping list, we try to find just the right thing for each person—something uniquely suited for them. We want to bless them with gifts they will enjoy. And it makes us happy when we see the joy in their faces as they open a gift that's perfect for them. Some people have a special knack for picking out just the right gift, but this season reminds us that God is the best Gift-Giver of all! "Thanks be to God for His indescribable gift!" we read in II Corinthians 9:15 (NIV). The very best gift God will ever give us, too wonderful for words, is the gift of eternal life through His Son, Jesus (see Romans 6:23). No other gift can compare to this!

God blesses our lives with many other gifts too. Everything good comes from Him, like the beauty of a quiet snowfall, the peace He gives us in our busy and challenging times, and a warm, safe place to call home. And He's also gifted each one of us with special talents and abilities. He created each of us to be unique, and He gave us special gifts that are as unique as we are. They are gifts we enjoy using, and God has given us these gifts for a reason—to serve others and glorify Him. As we use our unique gifts to bless others, we reflect God's love to the world in a way that only we can. In I Peter 4:10–11 (NLT), the apostle Peter talks about the importance of being a good steward of the gifts God gives us: "God has given each of you a gift from His great variety of spiritual gifts. Use them well to serve one another. Do you have the gift of speaking? Then speak as though God Himself were speaking through you. Do you have the gift of helping others? Do it with all the strength and energy that God supplies."

Each new day, let's be faithful in using the special gifts He's placed in us for His glory. And let's not forget that every day is a gift in itself, so let's embrace every moment! Having a peaceful, quiet time with God is always a great way to begin the day.

Today's recipe is Crumb Coffee Cake! As you mix the batter and prepare the crumb topping, thank God for the unique gifts and talents He's blessed you with and for all the good gifts He brings you throughout your days.

Lord, You're such a generous, loving Father, and You never stop pouring out Your goodness into our lives. Our days are blessed because of You. Every gift You give to us is good and perfect, and You always give us exactly what we need. We thank You and praise You for giving us the greatest Gift of all: the gift of everlasting life through Your Son, Jesus. It's a gift that fills our hearts with so much joy and hope, knowing we will have all of eternity with You. We are humbled and amazed at the depth of Your love for us and all You do for us. We're grateful for the unique gifts and abilities You've placed in us. We pray that we will always be faithful to use them to serve others well and glorify You. Help us to be good stewards and live our lives wisely and obediently as we follow Your leading. Amen.

crumb coffee cake

The glaze on top of this coffee cake is optional, but it makes a nice finishing touch!

PREP: 15 MIN. | COOK: 25 MIN. | TOTAL TIME: 40 MIN. | SERVINGS: 8–10

CRUMB TOPPING:

⅓ cup all-purpose baking mix

⅓ cup brown sugar, packed

½ teaspoon ground cinnamon

⅓ cup pecans, chopped

2 tablespoons butter, melted

COFFEE CAKE:

2½ cups all-purpose baking mix

1½ teaspoons ground cinnamon

¾ cup milk

⅓ cup sour cream

3 tablespoons sugar

1 large egg

1. Preheat oven to 350°F. Grease or line a 9-inch round pan with parchment paper; set aside.

2. In a small bowl, combine the dry ingredients for the Crumb Topping, then pour in the melted butter and mix everything with a fork until crumbly; set aside.

3. In medium-size bowl, mix together the baking mix, cinnamon, milk, sour cream, sugar, and egg, mixing well.

4. Pour batter into prepared pan and sprinkle evenly with the Crumb Topping.

5. Bake for 25 minutes, or until toothpick inserted in center comes out clean. Let cool in pan completely.

OPTIONAL SIMPLE GLAZE: To add a simple glaze on top, mix together ½ cup powdered sugar and 1 to 1½ tablespoons milk. Drizzle over the top of the cake after it has cooled and let set. Then slice and serve.

looking forward with hope

The One who is the true light, who gives light to everyone, was coming into the world.
JOHN 1:9 NLT

When we hope for something, it's usually for outcomes we want: a larger home, a new opportunity, or safety when we're traveling. There's also the kind of hope the Bible teaches about. Biblical hope is defined as confidently expecting what God has promised us. We can find this kind of hope in the story of Jesus' birth.

Throughout the Old Testament, we find passages telling about the coming of the Messiah. The Jewish people, under Roman rule, were looking forward with anticipation to a King of their own who would free them. In Jeremiah 33:15 (NLT) God said: "I will raise up a righteous descendant from King David's line." Matthew 1:6–17 shows the fulfillment of this, recording the lineage of King David to Jesus. There are Scriptures that even point to the birthplace of Jesus: "Bethlehem Ephrathah, though you are small among the clans of Judah, out of you will come for Me one who will be ruler over Israel" (Micah 5:2 NIV). Bethlehem was the smallest town in Judah at the time Jesus was born, a humble place of birth for a King, but that was part of God's plan. This reminds us that God works in mysterious ways. Even when God is doing something that doesn't make sense to us, we still know that He is working everything out according to His plan and for our good.

The words found in Isaiah 9:2, 6 (NLT) are also filled with hope: "The people who walk in darkness will see a great light. . . . For a Child is born to us, a Son is given to us. The government will rest on His shoulders. And He will be called: Wonderful Counselor, Mighty God, Everlasting Father, Prince of Peace." The Jews were looking for a King to rule with righteousness, and God sent His Son, Jesus to give all of humanity "the light that leads to life" (John 8:12 NLT).

The Bible is full of God's promises to us—to love us, care for us, guide us, provide for us, and give us hope and peace, no matter the challenges we face. Knowing that we can count on God to keep these promises (and so many more), helps us find the strength to keep going on busy or overwhelming days. It renews us so we can continue to look forward to all He has for us. We can live each day in hopeful anticipation of good and sometimes mysterious things to come.

Today's recipe is Apple-Cranberry Muffins. Enjoy the flavors of fresh, chopped apples and cranberries—they go so well together! As the muffins bake, think about the anticipation of that first bite—fluffy, tart, and full of delight. And yet, even that eager moment pales in comparison to the hope-filled, heart-stirring anticipation of the coming of the King.

We . . . wait with eager hope
for the day when God will give us our full rights
as His adopted children. . . .
We were given this hope when we were saved.
ROMANS 8:23-24 NLT

The gift of God is eternal life in Christ Jesus our Lord.
ROMANS 6:23 NIV

Let us hold unswervingly to the hope we profess,
for He who promised is faithful.
HEBREWS 10:23 NIV

Rejoice that the Lord Jesus has become your strength
and your song—He has become your salvation.
CHARLES SPURGEON

We . . . can have great confidence as we hold
to the hope that lies before us.
HEBREWS 6:18 NLT

apple-cranberry muffins

The flavors of apple and cranberry are wonderful to enjoy this time of year— and baking these muffins will make your kitchen feel warm and cozy!

PREP: 20 MIN. | COOK: 18–20 MIN. | TOTAL TIME: 40 MIN. | SERVINGS: 14–15

- 2 cups all-purpose flour
- ½ cup granulated sugar
- ⅓ teaspoon salt
- 1 tablespoon baking powder
- 1 teaspoon cinnamon
- ¼ teaspoon cloves
- ¼ teaspoon nutmeg
- 1 large egg at room temperature, beaten
- ¼ cup butter, melted
- 1 cup milk at room temperature
- 1 cup apples, finely chopped
- 1 cup fresh or frozen cranberries, chopped

1. Preheat oven to 350°F. Line two muffin pans with 14 to 15 paper liners; set aside.
2. In a large bowl, add flour, sugar, salt, baking powder, cinnamon, cloves, and nutmeg; blend everything well.
3. In medium-size bowl, mix together the egg, melted butter, and milk. Add this mixture to the dry ingredients in the large bowl, mixing everything until just combined.
4. Stir chopped apples and cranberries into the batter, mixing until apples and cranberries are evenly incorporated.
5. Spoon batter into the lined muffin cups until they are between ⅔ and ¾ full. Bake for 18 to 20 minutes, until a toothpick inserted in the centers comes out clean. Let cool in muffin tins for 5 minutes, then remove muffins to wire rack to cool a little more. Serve warm with butter or whipped cream cheese. Or cool completely and serve later.

perfect peace

*Glory to God . . .
and on earth peace to those
on whom His favor rests.*

LUKE 2:14 NIV

We never tire of reading or hearing the passage from Luke 2 during the Christmas season. The heavenly host of angels appears to the shepherds watching their flocks in the field at night and proclaims, "Glory to God in the highest heaven, and on earth peace to those on whom His favor rests." Peace really did come to earth that night because Jesus Himself is our peace (see Ephesians 2:14). He is our Source of inner peace, and to those who have faith and trust in Him, He gives us His peace "at all times and in every way" (II Thessalonians 3:16 NIV).

It's a peace that is beyond our comprehension or understanding—a perfect peace that only God can give to us. It calms our hearts and gives us strength to get through anything that comes our way. It soothes and quiets our minds as we focus on God, His truth, and His promises instead of our worries and fears. Philippians 4:7 (TLB) tells us, "God's peace . . . is far more wonderful than the human mind can understand. His peace will keep your thoughts and your hearts quiet and at rest as you trust in Christ Jesus." In Isaiah 9:6 Jesus is called the Prince of Peace—and because of the peace we have through Him, we can walk through even the most difficult circumstances.

At the Last Supper, Jesus knew His disciples would be facing many trials, and He promised them His peace would be with them: "I am leaving you with a gift—peace of mind and heart! And the peace I give isn't fragile like the peace the world gives" (John 14:27 TLB). He calls His peace a gift—and it's a gift He gives us too. He wants to pour out His perfect peace into our lives to strengthen and sustain us. Whatever trials we face, we can have this peace every day because it's found in Jesus. He is always with us and will always be our peace (see Micah 5:5).

We could probably all use a little more peace and calm as we go through each day, couldn't we? Whenever you can, take some time out for *you* and enjoy some quiet. Or do something relaxing that soothes and calms your soul. Maybe it's sitting in a comfy chair with a cup of hot chocolate or maybe it's wrapping up in a blanket to sit on the porch swing and watch the world go by. Whatever it may be, invite Jesus into that space with you today, and thank Him for the perfect peace He brings to your heart, mind, and soul.

Maybe the process of preparing food brings you peace. If so, the act of chopping vegetables and mixing ingredients in today's recipe could help you quiet your mind. Plus, the Million Dollar Dip is tasty and easy to make—it's sure to be a family favorite.

Lord, there is so much to treasure in Your Word. We love to read about that glorious night when the shepherds heard the Good News of Jesus' birth— a Savior bringing the indescribable gift of salvation. The Gift of all gifts. And You give us so many other gifts. You're our Prince of Peace, bringing us Your perfect peace, too wonderful for us to fully understand. We thank You for this peace that comforts us, renews us, and strengthens us. It's a peace that we can always have. There's never a time when we need to be without it, because You are always with us, step by step, throughout our days. When we start feeling anxious, remind us that we can release all our worries to You. Help us remember to focus on Your truth and promises so we can rest in Your peace. We're grateful for Your amazing love for us and all the ways You bless us. Amen.

million dollar dip

If you want this dip to have a thinner consistency, stir in a little extra mayonnaise or a tablespoon or two of half-and-half or heavy whipping cream.

PREP: 15 MIN. | COOK: 0 MIN. | TOTAL TIME: 15 MIN. | SERVINGS: 8–10

1½ cups mayonnaise

1 (8-ounce) package cream cheese, softened

½ teaspoon garlic powder

Optional: dash of cayenne pepper and paprika

2 cups (8 ounces) shredded sharp cheddar cheese

4 green onions, thinly sliced

⅔ cup real bacon bits or pieces, or cooked and crumbled bacon

½ cup slivered almonds

1. In a medium-size bowl, mix the mayonnaise and cream cheese, blending well. Then mix in the garlic powder and dashes of cayenne pepper and paprika, if using.

2. Add in the shredded cheese, green onions, bacon, and almonds. Mix everything together until well combined.

3. Serve immediately in a dip bowl or chill in the refrigerator until ready to serve.

4. Serve with your favorite crackers, corn or tortilla chips, pretzels, and/or raw veggies. You can also use this as a spread on celery sticks or bagels, or as a topping on a baked potato!

great joy

**I bring you good news that
will cause great joy for all the people.**

LUKE 2:10 NIV

It's the time of year we celebrate our Savior's birth and sing our favorite Christmas songs. "Joy to the World" is one of the most popular hymns of the season. Written in 1719 by Isaac Watts, it wasn't intended to be a Christmas hymn, but a century after he wrote it, it was set to music and released during the Christmas holiday—and it has become a favorite song this time of year. Watts found his inspiration from Psalm 98: "The LORD has made His salvation known. . . . He has remembered His love and His faithfulness to Israel. . . . Shout for joy to the LORD, all the earth, burst into jubilant song with music. . . . Let the sea resound . . . the world, and all who live in it" (verses 2–3, 7 NIV). This joyful psalm speaks of how all the earth celebrates Jesus and the salvation we have through Him. It led Watts to write these words of celebration in his hymn: "Joy to the world, the Lord is come! / Let earth receive her King / Let every heart prepare Him room / And heaven and nature sing."

As we look back on the story of Jesus' birth, we can find joy in remembering the announcement of the angel to shepherds: "I bring you good news that will bring great joy to all people. The Savior—yes, the Messiah, the Lord—has been born today in Bethlehem" (Luke 2:10–11 NLT). And we can find joy in Jesus in our present moments, too, as we spend time with Him. His joy brings us strength, peace, and hope—the complete fullness of joy only He can give. Even in hard times we can have joy, because the joy we have is through Him and isn't dependent on our circumstances. Romans 12:12 (NIV) tells us, "Be joyful in hope, patient in affliction, faithful in prayer." Our joy is found in Jesus, not in what is happening around us.

Are you feeling joyful today? Or are you feeling tired and underappreciated? Does the busyness of the holiday season tend to wear you down? With so many presents to buy and so many activities to participate in, it's easy to get overwhelmed and lose our joy—we start going through the motions, not really pausing to reflect on the joy that fills our hearts on a daily basis. Take a moment today to close your eyes, focus on Jesus, and allow His presence to fill you with true joy. You can even hum the song, letting the lyrics take root—joy to the world, the Lord has come!

Another way to bring joy back to your holiday season is to host a get-together. And today's recipe is perfect for any holiday gathering. The Charcuterie Snack Board is filled with so many good things. Invite your loved ones over to share this with, and while they are there, remind them of the joy we find in Jesus. Discuss how the busyness of this season can get to all of us, and lean on each other for encouragement.

Consider it pure joy . . .
whenever you face trials of many kinds,
because you know that the testing of your
faith produces perseverance.
JAMES 1:2–3 NIV

The joy of the Lord is your strength.
NEHEMIAH 8:10 NIV

Joy is the serious business of Heaven.
C. S. LEWIS

Rejoice in the Lord always.
I will say it again: Rejoice!
PHILIPPIANS 4:4 NIV

Let the trees of the forest sing for joy
before the Lord, for He is coming!
PSALM 96:12–13 NLT

Though you do not see Him now, you trust Him;
and you rejoice with a glorious, inexpressible joy.
The reward for trusting Him
will be the salvation of your souls.
I PETER 1:8–9 NLT

charcuterie snack board

Use extra bowls or plates, if needed, for any additional dips or snack items and place them next to your charcuterie board.

PREP: 30 MIN. | COOK: 0 MIN. | TOTAL TIME: 30 MIN. | SERVINGS: 8

2 kinds of cheese, sliced

Crackers or baguette slices

6 to 7 kinds of fruit and vegetables, (e.g., grapes, strawberries, sliced oranges, cherry tomatoes, sliced cucumbers, olives, baby carrots)

1 (6-ounce) package dried apricots or other dried fruit

1½ cups nuts (e.g., mixed nuts, almonds, or cashews)

1 or 2 kinds of dip (e.g., ranch dip, hummus, or fruit dip)

Optional: salami or smoked sausage slices

1. Line your charcuterie board with wax paper liner or parchment paper.
2. Fill a small bowl with dip and place on the board in the center or slightly off-center.
3. Arrange the rest of the snack items around the small bowl of dip in sections, starting from the bowl to the edge of the board, like a sun ray. Or have fun creating your own unique arrangement!

perfect love

This is how God showed His love among us: He sent His one and only Son into the world that we might live through Him.
I JOHN 4:9 NIV

When you think of the word *love*, what is the first thing that pops in your head? Is it that rom-com movie you love? Maybe you think of red hearts and pink flowers. Or maybe you think of your spouse or significant other and a romantic time that swept you off your feet. While all of these symbolize the word *love*, none compare to the definition of the word *love*. The definition of *love* is *Jesus* (I John 4:16). Love is His very nature. His love for us is unconditional, unchanging, faithful, and everlasting. It's also immeasurable—so much wider and longer and higher and deeper than we can comprehend (see Ephesians 3:18). And we have the peace and joy of knowing that nothing can ever separate us from His love (see Romans 8:38–39). We are always in His constant love and care, and nothing can ever change that.

For some, the holiday season can bring a sense of loneliness with it. It can remind you of fractured relationships that used to be whole, loved ones who have passed on, and times when it seemed as if life was better. This year, as these hard memories start to flood your mind, remember that you can count on God's love to encourage, strengthen, and hold you. The love you felt in past relationships and in easier times is the same love you have today. He is love. He was there then, and He is there now. There's a chapter in the Bible that describes what love is: "Love is patient, love is kind. It . . . rejoices with the truth. It always protects, always trusts, always hopes, always perseveres. Love never fails" (I Corinthians 13:4, 6–8 NIV). This passage helps us understand how God loves us, and it also shows us how He wants us to love others. We can learn from His example: "Watch what God does, and then you do it. . . . Keep company with Him and learn a life of love. . . . His love was not cautious but extravagant. He didn't love in order to get something from us but to give everything of Himself to us. Love like that" (Ephesians 5:1–2 THE MESSAGE). As we look to Him, He will show us how we can be beautiful expressions of His love to others.

Today's recipe was chosen to bring you comfort during the chilly winter months. This hearty Loaded Baked-Potato Soup is a cozy embrace in a bowl. As you enjoy each spoonful, remember how greatly you are loved by God. He loves you more than you can know, and His comforting presence is always with you.

Lord, Your perfect love for us is such a gift. We're amazed at all the love You pour into our lives. It's hard for us to comprehend how great Your love is, but we are so grateful for it. We thank You for giving us the greatest Gift we could ever receive through Your Son, Jesus, and that nothing can ever separate us from Your love. Help us to love others the way You love us as we learn from You. Let us be Your hands and feet to those around us, showing and sharing Your love. And let us grow in our faithfulness in spending time with You in Your Word and drawing near to You each day. We thank You that You are never, ever too busy to spend time with us. We're so grateful for Your love, grace, and goodness in our lives, and we love You and praise You for that. Amen.

loaded baked potato soup

To save time, you can substitute purchased pre-cooked real bacon pieces for the cooked and crumbled bacon.

PREP: 40 MIN. | COOK: 20 MIN. | TOTAL TIME: 60 MIN. | SERVINGS: 8–10

- 1 cup cooked and crumbled bacon (about 16 slices), divided
- ½ cup (1 stick) butter
- ⅓ cup all-purpose flour
- 1½ cups half-and-half
- 5 cups chicken broth
- 4 large russet potatoes, peeled and cubed
- 1 cup sliced green onions, divided
- ½ teaspoon salt
- ¼ teaspoon pepper
- 2 cups sour cream, divided
- 2 cups shredded cheddar cheese, divided

1. Cook bacon in a large skillet until crispy; drain on paper towel and let cool, then crumble and set aside (or use pre-cooked real bacon pieces).

2. In a large pot, melt butter over medium heat, then stir in the flour and mix until smooth. Gradually stir in the half-and-half and then the chicken broth, stirring constantly for several minutes.

3. Add the cubed, uncooked potatoes, ½ cup of the sliced green onions, and the salt and pepper to the mixture in the pot; bring to a boil, then reduce heat and simmer, uncovered, for 20 minutes, or until potatoes are tender (stir occasionally while soup is cooking). For a thicker, creamier soup, mash at least half of the potatoes right in the pot. Then stir in 1 cup of the sour cream, 1 cup of the cheddar cheese, and ½ cup of the crumbled bacon.

4. Continue to simmer and stir mixture until the cheese is melted, then serve. Use the remaining crumbled bacon, green onion, sour cream, and cheddar cheese as toppings.

a warm welcome

> Above all, love each other deeply. . . .
> Offer hospitality to one another.
>
> I PETER 4:8-9 NIV

As we spend more time inside during the winter season, enjoying the warmth of our homes, it could be a good opportunity to practice hospitality. Many of us feel intimidated by the idea of opening our homes to others. We worry that our homes aren't roomy enough, that our decorating isn't attractive enough, or that the food we serve won't be good enough. But *true* hospitality has nothing to do with any of this!

We often confuse hospitality with entertaining, but they're very different. *Entertaining* is about the house, the décor, and the menu—and we come away from this kind of event so impressed by the talented hostess. We admire everything about it, from the perfectly decorated home to the amazing food. *Hospitality*, on the other hand, is about welcoming family, friends, and neighbors into our *real* lives, no matter how high the laundry is piled on the couch or how messy our kitchen might be. It's about being authentic, not perfect. That takes some of the pressure off, doesn't it?

When we practice hospitality, the preparations aren't as important as the guests. We see an example of this in Luke 10:39–40, when Jesus was at the home of Mary and Martha. Martha was focused on the preparations, and Mary was focused on Jesus, the guest. True hospitality is about serving others and being together—building community around the table as we share a meal, make or deepen friendships, share what's on our hearts, and encourage each other.

Maybe you're in a busy season where you're not able to host a meal. For you, hospitality and community might look like having a simple cookie exchange and hot cocoa with neighbors one evening, meeting up with a friend for coffee to catch up, or volunteering to serve a meal to the homeless. All of this is hospitality—serving others in love.

No matter how you go about sharing hospitality with others, remember that God's love can shine through you to love others in a way they may have never been loved before. His love is powerful. It can break down walls and open doors, so don't be afraid to put yourself out there. Your hospitality may be a life-changing event.

If you are planning to open your home for the first time, today's recipe is a for-sure winner that everyone will love. Creamy Cheesy Potatoes is an easy side dish that is sure to put a smile on the faces of your guests.

Don't forget to show hospitality to strangers, for some who have done this have entertained angels without realizing it!
HEBREWS 13:2 NLT

When God's people are in need, be ready to help them. Always be eager to practice hospitality.
ROMANS 12:13 NLT

Whenever we have the opportunity, we should do good to everyone—especially to those in the family of faith.
GALATIANS 6:10 NLT

Hospitality should have no other nature than love.
HENRIETTA MEARS

Share what you have with others. God takes particular pleasure in acts of worship—a different kind of "sacrifice"— that take place in kitchen and workplace and on the streets.
HEBREWS 13:16 THE MESSAGE

"Anyone who welcomes you welcomes Me, and anyone who welcomes Me welcomes the One who sent Me."
MATTHEW 10:40 NIV

creamy cheesy potatoes

These may be the creamiest mashed potatoes you'll ever make!

PREP: 30 MIN. | COOK: 30 MIN. | TOTAL TIME: 60 MIN. | SERVINGS: 12

3 pounds potatoes, peeled and cut into chunks

3 tablespoons milk

¾ teaspoon salt

½ teaspoon onion powder or garlic powder

¼ teaspoon pepper

4 tablespoons butter, divided

¾ cup sour cream

4 ounces cream cheese, softened

3 tablespoons fresh chives, chopped (or substitute 3 teaspoons dried chives)

1¾ to 2 cups shredded cheddar cheese, divided

¾ to 1 cup round buttery crackers, crushed

1. Preheat oven to 350°F. Grease a 9 x 13-inch baking pan; set aside.

2. In a medium-size pot, cook peeled and cut potatoes in salted water until tender, then drain.

3. In a large bowl, add potatoes, milk, salt, onion or garlic powder, pepper, and 2 tablespoons of the butter; mash potatoes with these ingredients, then mix with a large spoon until blended.

4. Add the sour cream, cream cheese, and chives, mixing until mixture is creamy. Then fold in 1 cup of the shredded cheddar cheese and stir until evenly blended.

5. Pour or spoon mixture evenly into greased baking pan. Combine the remaining 2 tablespoons butter with the crushed cracker crumbs, then sprinkle over the potatoes. Bake, uncovered, for 30 minutes. Top with the remaining ¾ to 1 cup shredded cheddar cheese the last 10 minutes of baking. Remove from oven, let cool a few minutes, then serve.

a generous heart

*Be rich in good works and generous to those in need,
always being ready to share with others.*
I TIMOTHY 6:17–18 NLT

We can all think of someone who has blessed us with their generosity at one time or another Maybe it was a good friend, a family member, or someone from church. Or it could have been an anonymous giver or someone we didn't know very well. When we are blessed by the generosity of someone, it fills us with thankfulness. We're so grateful for what they have freely, thoughtfully, and even sacrificially given to us . . . and for the time they took to go out of their way to notice and provide for our needs. And we give thanks to God for bringing these people into our lives. They've shown us God's love through their generous hearts.

Being blessed by a generous giver inspires and reminds us to give generously too—to be there for others, like those who have been there for us. It also reminds us of God's generosity in our lives—how He has blessed us with everything we have, and how His blessings continue to flow from His hand, filling our lives with His goodness and grace. Out of His overflow of goodness to us, we can pass blessings on to others. In II Corinthians 9:8, 11 (NIV) we're told, "God is able to bless you abundantly, so that in all things at all times, having all that you need, you will abound in every good work. . . . You will be enriched in every way so that you can be generous on every occasion, and . . . your generosity will result in thanksgiving to God." God equips us with all that we need to help others, and as we do that, we share God's love with them and glorify Him.

We often think of generosity as contributing money to a need or cause, but there are many other ways we can give generously to others: through our time, our encouragement, our help, our comfort, our giftings, our care, and our prayers. We can give what we have and what we are able to—whatever God has supplied us with—to bless someone else. God loves cheerful givers, and He wants us to give joyfully, and lovingly, the way He gives to us: "If you are really eager to give, then it isn't important how much you have to give. God wants you to give what you have, not what you haven't" (II Corinthians 8:12 TLB).

So let's give with generous hearts in whatever ways God is leading us to: providing a helping hand, sharing needed groceries, or making an encouraging phone call. If you're wanting to provide a meal for someone, Turkey Tetrazzini is a delicious way to bless their day. It's an easy spaghetti dish with a cheesy and creamy mushroom sauce, and it makes a heartwarming dinner. While you're preparing the sauce and pouring the mixture into your baking dish, reflect on the ways others have blessed you—and how you've seen God's love through their generosity!

Lord, You are so good and gracious to us. We are humbled by the generous ways You bless us and show us Your love. We thank You for the caring people You bring into our lives to help us on our journey. Through them, we see Your love and are reminded that You are with us, watching over us, and bringing the help we need to get through our challenging days and seasons. We see Your goodness through these generous hearts, and we are so blessed and thankful. Help us to grow in generosity, too, Father. We want to learn from You and follow the ways of Your generosity. You bless us so abundantly, and we want to share those blessings with others. Let us be bright reflections of You as You show us how to help others in the best way. Help us always to be cheerful, joyful givers to those around us. We thank You for Your loving example and pray that we will grow to be more like You. Amen.

turkey tetrazzini

You can substitute cheddar cheese for the mozzarella cheese if you prefer.

PREP: 25 MIN. | COOK: 35-40 MIN. | TOTAL TIME: 1 HR. 5 MIN. | SERVINGS: 8-10

- 1 (16-ounce) package of spaghetti
- 2 (10.5-ounce) cans condensed cream of mushroom soup, undiluted
- 1 cup sour cream
- ⅓ cup butter, melted
- 1 cup chicken broth
- ½ teaspoon salt
- ¼ teaspoon pepper
- ¾ cup onion, chopped
- 1 (8-ounce) can sliced mushrooms, drained
- 2 cups shredded mozzarella cheese, divided
- 3½ cups cooked turkey, chopped
- ¼ cup shredded Parmesan cheese

1. Preheat oven to 350°F. Grease or spray a 3- or 4-quart casserole dish or 9 x 13-inch pan; set aside.

2. Cook spaghetti or linguine according to package directions (before cooking, you can break noodles in half if desired); drain, then put cooked noodles in a large bowl and set aside.

3. In a medium-size bowl, mix together the condensed soup, sour cream, melted butter, chicken broth, salt, pepper, chopped onion, sliced mushrooms, and 1½ cups of the mozzarella cheese; stir everything together well. Then add this mixture to the cooked noodles in the large bowl, along with the chopped turkey, stirring until everything is combined.

4. Pour mixture into prepared baking dish; sprinkle top of casserole with the remaining ½ cup mozzarella and Parmesan cheeses. Bake, uncovered, for 35 to 40 minutes or until bubbly and heated through. Let cool a few minutes, then serve.

for His glory

**Whether you eat or drink or whatever you do,
do it all for the glory of God.**
I CORINTHIANS 10:31 NIV

During the winter season, the end of the year comes up much too quickly, and a new year is just on the horizon. We wonder how it's possible for the year to have gone by so fast. Where did the time go? We often look back on the things we did during the year. Did we accomplish what we wanted to? Did we check fun things off our bucket lists? Did we learn something new? Did we create special memories with the people we love? Here's something else we could reflect on: How did we grow in our faith and bring God glory during the year?

Paul told the early Christians in I Corinthians 10:31 that in everything they did, even the smallest everyday things like eating and drinking, to do it all for the glory of God. In other words, honor Him in all things, even the smallest of things. God created us to bring Him glory in every part of our lives and through the things we do and say: "All who claim Me as their God . . . I have made them for My glory. It was I who created them" (Isaiah 43:7 NLT). When we think about all God does for us—how He loves us, protects us, guides us, helps us, comforts us, and blesses us—we can't help but want to give Him glory.

There are many ways we can honor God and give Him glory as we go through our days and seasons. When we seek His guidance and wisdom in prayer and in our Bible reading, we show our reliance on Him and our trust in Him—that brings Him glory. Living life with a thankful heart and a positive attitude gives Him glory. When we worship Him, use the gifts He's blessed us with to serve others, and work at whatever we do with all our heart (see Colossians 3:23), we glorify Him. When we reflect His love, goodness, and grace to others, we bring glory to Him. When we see Him work in our lives and in the lives of others and praise Him for all He is doing, that brings Him glory. As we continue to grow in our relationship with Him, becoming more like Him, we are glorifying Him. And when we show the fruit of the Spirit in our lives—like patience and forgiveness—or learn from the hard experiences we go through, that brings Him glory too.

As we look forward to the coming year, let's keep it on our minds and hearts to bring glory to God through the things we do. Because it is only when we align our actions with God's plan for us that we are able to tap in to His deep well of meaning and peace.

Tip: Food gifts are a great way to spread joy and let others know they're in our thoughts! Graham Cracker Toffee is a sweet treat that everyone loves, and you can easily package it up in treat bags, tied with a holiday ribbon. You could even write an encouraging note to go with each treat bag you give. It's a sweet way to show others you are thinking of them!

May He fulfill by His power all your desire for goodness and complete your work of faith. In this way the name of our Lord Jesus will receive glory from you.
II THESSALONIANS 1:11–12 GNT

To You alone, O Lord, to You alone, and not to us, must glory be given because of Your constant love and faithfulness.
PSALM 115:1 GNT

For everything comes from God alone. Everything lives by His power, and everything is for His glory. To Him be glory evermore.
ROMANS 11:36 TLB

God is most glorified in us when we are most satisfied in Him.
JOHN PIPER

"Your abundant growth and your faithfulness as My followers will bring glory to the Father."
JOHN 15:8 THE VOICE

Worthy are You, O God, to receive glory and honor and power. You alone created all things, and through Your will and by Your design, they exist and were created.
REVELATION 4:11 THE VOICE

graham cracker toffee

This toffee can be stored in an airtight container for up to ten days.

PREP: 25 MIN. | COOK: 8 MIN. | TOTAL TIME: 33 MIN. | SERVINGS: 8–10

14 full-size graham crackers

1 cup (2 sticks) salted butter

1 cup light brown sugar, firmly packed

2 cups semisweet chocolate chips

½ teaspoon pure vanilla extract

¼ cup pecans, chopped

¼ cup toffee bits

Optional: 1 to 2 tablespoons sprinkles

1. Preheat oven to 350°F. Line a 10 x 15-inch rimmed baking sheet with parchment paper.

2. Place graham crackers in a single layer, lying flat, over the entire baking sheet.

3. In a medium-size saucepan, combine butter and brown sugar over medium heat and bring to a boil. Boil for 3½ to 4 minutes, stirring constantly as mixture thickens.

4. Remove from heat, stir in the vanilla extract, and immediately pour mixture over the graham crackers; spread mixture evenly to cover the crackers completely.

5. Bake for 7 to 8 minutes, until edges are bubbly. Remove from oven and sprinkle evenly with the semisweet chocolate chips. Let sit for 4 to 5 minutes, giving the chocolate chips time to melt, then spread the melted chocolate evenly over the crackers.

6. Sprinkle melted chocolate with the chopped pecans and toffee bits. Add some sprinkles too, if desired.

7. Cool completely until chocolate sets, about 1 to 2 hours, then break into pieces. To cool the chocolate more quickly, put the pan of toffee in the refrigerator for 30 to 60 minutes.

wait patiently

**If we must keep trusting God
for something that hasn't happened yet,
it teaches us to wait patiently and confidently.**

ROMANS 8:25 TLB

We live in a world of instant gratification, where we don't like to wait. When we decide we want something, we want it *now*. If there are delays, we get impatient. We often feel the same way when we're waiting on God for something, perhaps to answer prayer or provide help in a tough situation. But even when it doesn't look like anything is happening while we're waiting, God is working. That's why we can wait *patiently* and *confidently* on Him. It's not easy, especially when we've been waiting a long time, but our waiting time is never wasted time. God can teach us, grow us, and prepare us as we wait.

We can see an example of how God grows and prepares us in our waiting time through the story of Moses. He had fled from Egypt to the desert of Midian after striking down an Egyptian (Exodus 2:11–15). He went from living in a palace of Egyptian royalty to becoming a shepherd in the wilderness for forty years. But these years were not wasted years. This was a time when God was preparing him to lead the Israelites out of Egypt and toward the promised land. In those forty years, Moses would learn to live simply and survive in the heat of the desert. His lessons learned from the humble work of shepherding animals would translate into shepherding and leading the Israelites on their journey. And it was in the quiet of the wilderness that God appeared to Moses in the flaming bush, telling him, "I am sending you . . . to bring My people the Israelites out of Egypt (Exodus 3:10 NIV). God always works in our times of waiting, growing us and preparing us for our future seasons. We often don't understand why we're waiting, but we can trust that God has a purpose for our waiting time. As we wait patiently, our hope, faith, and trust grow stronger. "Patience develops strength of character in us and helps us trust God more each time we use it until finally our hope and faith are strong and steady" (Romans 5:4 TLB).

As we go through our waiting seasons, let's be faithful to wait well—with patience, trust, hope, and anticipation. Let's pray with persistence, worship with gratitude, learn from His teaching, and hold on to His promises. Let's embrace where we're at in the present, too, enjoying the moments of the season we're in right now.

One way to enjoy the present is with these rich, buttery Ginger Shortbread Cookies. Let each melt-in-your-mouth bite remind you of God's goodness and how He loves to richly bless us.

Lord, we praise You because You are in control of all things and Your plans and purposes are always good. Even when we can't understand how You are working, help us to remember that we can trust completely in Your perfect ways and timing. Forgive us for our impatience and keep us strong and steady so we never run ahead of You and what You are doing in our lives. Let us always remember that because You have good things planned for us, we can wait confidently on You for any of our needs in any situations we face. Let us grow in the ways You are wanting us to grow in our times of waiting. Give us wisdom in how You are guiding us and understanding in what You are teaching us. Thank You that our waiting times are never wasted—that You use them to prepare us for the new season ahead. We're grateful, Father, for all Your love and how You bless us, guide us, teach us, and walk with us every day. Amen.

ginger shortbread cookies

Store shortbread in an airtight container, placing sheets of parchment paper between layers.

PREP: 20 MIN. | COOK: 25 MIN. | TOTAL TIME: 45 MIN. | SERVINGS: 18

- 1 cup (2 sticks) unsalted butter, softened
- ¾ cup light brown sugar, packed
- 2¼ cups all-purpose flour
- 2½ teaspoons ground ginger
- ½ teaspoon ground cinnamon
- ½ teaspoon ground nutmeg
- 1 teaspoon pure vanilla extract
- Optional: Coarse decorating sugar or other sprinkles for sprinkling on top

1. Preheat oven to 350°F. Line the bottom of a 9 x 9-inch pan with parchment paper, extending it a few inches over the sides (so you can lift the shortbread out of the pan after baking).

2. In a large bowl, blend butter and brown sugar until creamy. Add the flour, ginger, cinnamon, nutmeg, and vanilla, and mix everything together (dough will be thick and crumbly).

3. Press dough firmly and evenly into the parchment-lined pan. Prick the surface of the dough with a fork, about 1 inch apart. If desired, sprinkle coarse decorating sugar on top.

4. Bake at for 25 minutes or until edges are lightly browned. Cool in pan for 5 minutes, then remove by lifting out with the edges of parchment paper and placing on a flat surface.

5. Cut shortbread into 3 rows by 3 rows with a long knife, to make 9 squares; then cut each square diagonally in half to make 18 triangles. Cool cookies completely (about 1 hour).

live in wonder

You are the God of miracles and wonders!
You still demonstrate Your awesome power.

PSALM 77:14 TLB

God is a God of wonders, and this world He created is full of wonders too! Sometimes we just get so busy we don't have time to slow down and notice them. Just waking up to a new day is a wonder: the gift of another breath and another chance to see the splendor of the sunrise or the beauty of swirling snowflakes falling gently from the sky. We see God's wonder not only in nature, but in other ways too—through miracles He has done in the past and through the wondrous ways He works in our lives today. David said in the Psalms, "Many, Lord my God, are the wonders You have done, the things You planned for us. None can compare with You; were I to speak and tell of Your deeds, they would be too many to declare" (Psalm 40:5 NIV). The wonders God has done are too numerous to count, and He continues to do more each day!

We read of God's wondrous works in ancient times, like the parting of the Red Sea as the Israelites fled Egypt (Exodus 14:21). And the events surrounding Jesus' birth were filled with so much wonder that the shepherds were glorifying God, and Mary "treasured up all these things and pondered them in her heart" (Luke 2:19 NIV). Most of all, the miracle and wonder of Jesus' resurrection continues to fill us with joy and hope in the promise of eternal life. God has been working wonders since time began. When we remember His "miracles of long ago" (Psalm 77:11 NIV), they remind us of His power and goodness and all that He can do today and in the future.

God delights in doing wondrous works in each one of our lives too. If you are in a season that feels hopeless and there doesn't seem to be a way out of this tough situation, He is always faithful to make a way. No situation is impossible for Him to work through. Ask God to guide you, help you, and restore you. He is the God of miracles. He may close a few doors, but it's usually to keep you moving in the right direction. Don't be discouraged, my friend. He is the Source of wonder and brings fullness and abundance to our lives. That gives us reason to celebrate His goodness all season long.

If you're planning any fun celebrations or just wanting to make something fun, Marshmallow Pops are a colorful, simple sweet treat to make. Just dip the marshmallows in melted wafers and fun sprinkles for a fun and colorful dessert. As you make these easy pops, look back on the wondrous ways God has worked in your life and think about how they made an impact on you. And enjoy the new wonders He brings your way each day!

I recall all You have done, O Lord;
I remember Your wonderful deeds of long ago.
They are constantly in my thoughts.
I cannot stop thinking about Your mighty works.
PSALM 77:11–12 NLT

O Sovereign Lord, You have only begun to show
Your greatness and the strength of Your hand to me.
DEUTERONOMY 3:24 NLT

Many will see what He has done and be amazed.
They will put their trust in the Lord.
PSALM 40:3 NLT

We have a God who delights in impossibilities.
BILLY SUNDAY

Blessed God, Israel's God,
the one and only wonder-working God!
Blessed always His blazing glory!
All earth brims with His glory.
PSALM 72:18 THE MESSAGE

Everything was created through Him and for Him.
He existed before anything else,
and He holds all creation together.
COLOSSIANS 1:16–17 NLT

marshmallow pops

You can package these pops in small cellophane bags for giving to others!

PREP: 40 MIN. | COOK: 0 MIN. | TOTAL TIME: 40 MIN. | SERVINGS: 45–50

Lollipop sticks

1 (12-ounce) bag regular-size marshmallows (or use jumbo or giant-size)

Valentine sprinkles (you can also use decorating sugar)

1 (10 or 12-ounce) package melting wafers (chocolate, white, or pink)

Kitchen items: small bowl(s) for sprinkles; 3 to 4 mugs for drying the pops, with candies used as filler to prop up the pops

Optional: small cellophane bags for gifting

1. Push a lollipop stick into the center of one of the edges of each marshmallow; set aside. Pour sprinkles into a small bowl. Fill mugs to be used for drying the pops with small candies.

2. Melt the melting wafers according to package directions.

3. After wafers are melted, dip each marshmallow, one at a time, into the melted chocolate, about halfway up; let excess chocolate drip off. Right after dipping each marshmallow, roll in the small bowl of sprinkles to cover some or all of the melted chocolate, then place marshmallow pop, stick down, in a mug until the chocolate sets.

4. Repeat for each marshmallow, placing in mugs to set. You can also put the mugs of marshmallow pops in the refrigerator for a few minutes so they'll set faster.

5. After chocolate is set, store pops in an airtight container or wrap each pop in a small cellophane bag for gifting.

THE CHANGING SEASONS:
winter-spring

As nature's winter rest gradually comes to an end, the fresh new life of springtime begins to emerge. We enjoyed our cozy winter days and found rest for our souls, spending times of quiet with the Lord. And we're thankful for other insights we gained in winter. We reflected on the good gifts God gives and His greatest Gift, Jesus. We remembered that our perfect peace and joy come from Him and not our circumstances, that He loves us with a perfect love, and that nothing can ever separate us from it. We learned that true hospitality is about serving others and being together, and that we can be generous in meaningful ways with our time, resources, encouragement, and prayers. We were reminded that whatever we do can bring God glory, that it's important to wait patiently on His timing, and that we can see His wonder in each new day and be filled with hope for all He will do in the future.

We're thankful for our time of rest and reflection in winter as we anticipate the coming of glorious spring. Soon we'll be seeing lighter, warmer days. The cycle of the seasons will begin again and remind us that God has a purpose for every season in nature. Springtime will bring new beginnings and new growth. Trees will bud, and the sun will warm the soil and ready it for planting. And just as nature, in the quiet of winter, has been preparing for the fresh, new season of spring, God has been preparing us for what He has ahead in this new season. We'll have new things to accomplish, new lessons to learn, new wonders to discover. God grows us as He teaches us with the textbook of each new season, and He writes beautiful new chapters in our life stories.

We look forward to the milder weather, the sweet taste of our favorite berries, flying kites, planting seeds in our gardens, and sharing fresh, simple meals with family and friends. When spring arrives, we will marvel at the miracle of new life and growth we'll soon see in nature and be reminded that creation is God's amazing handiwork; He spoke all this beauty into being for us to enjoy. And we know that He will continue to be there with us in every season, in the good times and the challenging times, holding us close each day. "I trust in You, Lord; I say, 'You are my God.' My times are in Your hands" (Psalm 31:14–15 NIV).

Spring is coming, and we are ready to experience all this season holds for us. The tree branches of winter are still bare but graceful, as we wait patiently for them to bud. All is quiet in nature, but the resting earth is starting to awaken, slowly getting ready to unfold all its beauty and life renewed. It's a miracle we never get tired of seeing. As we watch and wait for this season of new life, let's take time to notice the ways God works all around us to bring wonder to our world, and let's remember these hope-filled words from Matthew 19:16 (NIV) that refresh our souls and encourage us in all our seasons: "With God all things are possible."

Lord, we see Your goodness in every season, in the way You care for all of nature and in the way You care and provide for each one of us. The work of Your hands fills us with wonder. Everything about Your creation is amazing, from the stars in the sky that You know by name to the seas and everything in them. And Your thoughts of us outnumber the grains of sand! Heavenly Father, we're so grateful for Your gifts that make our lives full—Your perfect love, hope, and peace. And we thank You that You're with us in every season, teaching us, caring for us, and watching over us. You fill us with the rest and renewal we need—the deep rest for our souls—when we spend time with You. Every season is a gift from You, and we're so grateful for all the ways You work in all of our days. We love You and praise You for Your blessings and faithfulness. Amen.

recipe index

BREAKFAST

Apple-Cheddar Biscuits 110
Apple Baked Oatmeal 118
Apple-Cranberry Muffins 166
Blueberry Chip Muffins 62
Cherry-Almond Coffee Cake 66
Cranberry Quick Bread 158
Crumb Coffee Cake 162
Easy Cheese Danish 22
Honey-Almond Granola 18
Pumpkin Coffee Cake 114
Pumpkin-Pecan Bread 122
Spinach-Artichoke Strata 14

APPETIZERS AND SNACKS

Bacon-Ranch Cheese Ball 30
Berry Tarts 74
Caramel Apple Dip 130
Charcuterie Snack Board 174
7-Layer Dip 26
Loaded Baked Potato Dip 126
Million Dollar Dip 170
Stuffed Ranch Eggs 78
Veggie Pizza 70

SIDE DISHES

Apple-Pear Salad 134
Classic Potato Salad 82
Corn Casserole 138
Creamy Cheesy Potatoes 182
Refreshing Fruit Salad 34
Strawberry Spinach Salad 86

MAIN DISHES

Chicken Broccoli Rice
    Casserole 42
Easy Cobb Salad 38
Loaded Baked Potato Soup 178
Secret Ingredient Chili 142
Taco Pasta Salad 90
Turkey Tetrazzini 186

DESSERTS

Chocolate Chip Coconut
    Oatmeal Cookies 146
Chocolate Mint Brownies 102
Easter Egg Blondies 46
Easy Patriotic Cookies 94
Ginger Shortbread 194
Graham Cracker Toffee 190
Lemon-Filled Cupcakes 50
Marshmallow Pops 198
Mini Apple Bundt Cakes 150
Peach Cobbler Cake 98
Strawberry Crinkle Cookies 54

index of recipes and ingredients

A

Almonds
- Almonds, whole, Charcuterie Snack Board, 174
- Apple-Pear Salad, 134
- Cherry-Almond Coffee Cake, 66
- Honey-Almond Granola, 18
- Million Dollar Dip, 170
- Strawberry Spinach Salad, 86
- Almond extract, Cherry-Almond Coffee Cake, 66

Apples
- Apple Baked Oatmeal, 118
- Apple-Cheddar Biscuits, 110
- Apple cider vinegar, Apple-Pear Salad, 134
- Apple-Cranberry Muffins, 166
- Apple-Pear Salad, 134

Applesauce
- Mini Apple Bundt Cakes, 150
- Apple Baked Oatmeal, 118
- Apple juice, Mini Apple Bundt Cakes, 150
- Caramel Apple Dip, 130
- Mini Apple Bundt Cakes, 150
- Apricots, dried, Charcuterie Snack Board, 174
- Artichoke hearts, canned, Spinach-Artichoke Strata, 14

Avocado
- Easy Cobb Salad, 38
- Taco Pasta Salad, 90

B

Bacon
- Bacon, cooked and crumbled
  - Easy Cobb Salad, 38
  - Loaded Baked Potato Soup, 178
- Bacon pieces
  - Bacon-Ranch Cheese Ball, 30
  - Loaded Baked Potato Dip, 126
  - Million Dollar Dip, 170
- Bacon-Ranch Cheese Ball, 30

Baking mix
- Apple-Cheddar Biscuits, 110
- Cherry-Almond Coffee Cake, 66
- Crumb Coffee Cake, 162
- Beef, ground, Taco Pasta Salad, 90
- Berry Tarts, 74
- Black beans, canned, Secret Ingredient Chili, 142
- Blueberry Chip Muffins, 62

Blueberries, fresh
- Berry Tarts, 74
- Blueberry Chip Muffins, 62
- Blondies, Easter Egg, 46
- Bread, crusty, Spinach-Artichoke Strata, 14
- Broccoli florets, frozen, Chicken Broccoli Rice Casserole, 42
- Brownies, Chocolate Mint, 102
- Brownie mix, Chocolate Mint Brownies, 102

C

- Cadbury Mini Eggs, Easter Egg Blondies, 46

Cake mix
- Lemon, Lemon-Filled Cupcakes, 50
- Strawberry, Strawberry Crinkle Cookies, 54
- Yellow
  - Mini Apple Bundt Cakes, 150
  - Peach Cobbler Cake, 98
- Caramel or caramel bits, Caramel Apple Dip, 130
- Caramel Apple Dip, 130

Casseroles
- Chicken Broccoli Rice Casserole, 42
- Corn Casserole, 138
- Spinach-Artichoke Strata, 14
- Cashews, Charcuterie Snack Board, 174
- Catalina dressing, Taco Pasta Salad, 90
- Celery ribs, Classic Potato Salad, 82

Cereal and grains
- Honey-Almond Granola, 18
- Apple Baked Oatmeal, 118
- Charcuterie Snack Board, 174

Cheese
- Blue cheese, Easy Cobb Salad, 38
- Cheese, assorted and sliced, Charcuterie Snack Board, 174
- Cheddar cheese, shredded
  - Apple-Cheddar Biscuits, 110
  - Bacon-Ranch Cheese Ball, 30
  - Chicken Broccoli Rice Casserole, 42
  - Creamy Cheesy Potatoes, 182
  - 7-Layer Dip, 26
  - Loaded Baked Potato Dip, 126
  - Loaded Baked Potato Soup, 178
  - Million Dollar Dip, 170

Veggie Pizza, 70
Cream cheese
    Bacon-Ranch Cheese Ball, 30
    Berry Tarts, 74
    Chocolate Mint Brownies, 102
    Creamy Cheesy Potatoes, 182
    Easy Cheese Danish, 22
    Million Dollar Dip, 170
    Veggie Pizza, 70
Feta cheese, Strawberry Spinach Salad, 86
Mexican blend cheese, Taco Pasta Salad, 90
Monterey Jack cheese, Spinach-Artichoke Strata, 14
Mozzarella cheese, Turkey Tetrazzini, 186
Parmesan cheese
    Apple-Pear Salad, 134
    Turkey Tetrazzini, 186
Cherry-Almond Coffee Cake, 66
Cherry pie filling, Cherry-Almond Coffee Cake, 66
Chicken, chopped or shredded
    Chicken Broccoli Rice Casserole, 42
    Easy Cobb Salad, Chicken, 38
Chicken broth
    Chicken Broccoli Rice Casserole, 42
    Loaded Baked Potato Soup, 178
    Turkey Tetrazzini, 186
Chicken Broccoli Rice Casserole, 42
Chocolate
    Cadbury Mini Eggs, Easter Egg Blondies, 46
    Chocolate Chip Coconut Oatmeal Cookies, 146
    Chocolate Mint Brownies, 102
    Mint chocolate chips, Chocolate Mint Brownies, 146
    Semisweet chocolate baking bars, Easy Patriotic Cookies, 94
    Semisweet chocolate chips
        Chocolate Chip Coconut Oatmeal Cookies, 146
        Graham Cracker Toffee, 190
    White chocolate baking bars, Easy Patriotic Cookies, 94
    White chocolate chips, Blueberry Chip Muffins, 62
Chocolate Chip Coconut Oatmeal Cookies, 146
Chocolate Mint Brownies, 102
Classic Potato Salad, 82

Cookies
    Chocolate Chip Coconut Oatmeal Cookies, 146
    Easy Patriotic Cookies, 94
    Ginger Shortbread Cookies, 194
    Strawberry Crinkle Cookies, 54
Coconut flakes, sweetened, Chocolate Chip Coconut Oatmeal Cookies, 146
Coconut oil, Chocolate Chip Coconut Oatmeal Cookies, 146
Coffee cake
    Cherry-Almond Coffee Cake, 66
    Crumb Coffee Cake, 162
    Pumpkin Coffee Cake, 114
Corn
    Corn Casserole, 138
    Corn, cream-style canned, Corn Casserole, 138
    Corn muffin mix, Corn Casserole, 138
    Corn, whole-kernel canned, Corn Casserole, 138
Cranberry
    Cranberries, dried, Apple-Pear Salad, 134
    Cranberries, fresh, Apple-Cranberry Muffins, 166
    Cranberries, fresh or frozen, Cranberry Quick Bread, 158
Crackers, buttery round
    Chicken Broccoli Rice Casserole, 42
    Creamy Cheesy Potatoes, 182
Cranberry Quick Bread, 158
Cream of chicken soup, condensed, Chicken Broccoli Rice Casserole, 42
Creamy Cheesy Potatoes, 182
Crumb Coffee Cake, 162

D

Dessert shells, Berry Tarts, 74
Dips
    Caramel Apple Dip, 130
    Dips, assorted, Charcuterie Snack Board, 174
    7-Layer Dip, 26
    Loaded Baked Potato Dip, 126
    Million Dollar Dip, 170

E

Easter Egg Blondies, 46
Easy Cheese Danish, 22
Easy Cobb Salad, 38
Easy Patriotic Cookies, 94

Eggs, hard-boiled
- Classic Potato Salad, 82
- Easy Cobb Salad, 38
- Stuffed Ranch Eggs, 78

F

Frosting, mint, Chocolate Mint Brownies, 102

Fruit
- Blueberries, fresh, Berry Tarts, 74
- Cantaloupe, Refreshing Fruit Salad, 34
- Cranberries, dried, Apple-Pear Salad, 134
- Cranberries, fresh, Apple-Cranberry Muffins, 166
- Fruit, assorted, Charcuterie Snack Board, 174
- Fruit Salad, Refreshing, 34
- Golden raisins, Honey-Almond Granola, 18
- Green seedless grapes, Refreshing Fruit Salad, 34
- Honeydew, Refreshing Fruit Salad, 34
- Lemon zest, Lemon-Filled Cupcakes, 50
- Mandarin oranges, canned, Refreshing Fruit Salad, 34
- Pears, chopped or sliced, Apple-Pear Salad, 134
- Peaches, canned, Peach Cobbler Cake, 98
- Pineapple chunks, Refreshing Fruit Salad, 34
- Raspberries, fresh, Berry Tarts, 74
- Strawberries
  - Refreshing Fruit Salad, 34
  - Strawberry Spinach Salad, 86
  - Refreshing Fruit Salad, 34

G

Glaze
- Cherry-Almond Coffee Cake, 66
- Easy Cheese Danish, 22

Graham crackers
- Graham Cracker Toffee, 190
- Ginger Shortbread Cookies, 194

H

Herbs
- Chives, fresh or dried
  - Apple-Cheddar Biscuits, 110
  - Creamy Cheesy Potatoes, 182
  - Stuffed Ranch Eggs, 78
- Cilantro, Taco Pasta Salad, 90

Honey-Almond Granola, 18

J

Jam, blueberry or raspberry, Berry Tarts, 74

L

7-Layer Dip, 26
Lemon curd, Lemon-Filled Cupcakes, 50
Lemon-Filled Cupcakes, 50
Loaded Baked Potato Dip, 126
Loaded Baked Potato Soup, 178
Lollipop sticks, Marshmallow Pops, 198

M

Marshmallows, Marshmallow Pops, 198
Marshmallow Pops, 198
Melting wafers, Marshmallow Pops, 198
Million Dollar Dip, 170
Mini Apple Bundt Cakes, 150
Mint extract, Chocolate Mint Brownies, 102
Muffins
- Apple-Cranberry Muffins, 166
- Blueberry Chip Muffins, 62

Mushrooms, canned, Turkey Tetrazzini, 186

N

Nuts, mixed, Charcuterie Snack Board, 174

O

Oats
- Old-fashioned oats
  - Apple Baked Oatmeal, 118
  - Honey-Almond Granola, 18
- Quick-cooking oats, Chocolate Chip Coconut Oatmeal Cookies, 146

Olive oil
- Apple-Pear Salad, 134
- Honey-Almond Granola, 18
- Spinach-Artichoke Strata, 14

Orange juice, Cranberry Quick Bread, 158
Orange extract, Cranberry Quick Bread, 158

P

Pasta
- Rotini (spiral) pasta, Taco Pasta Salad, 90
- Spaghetti, Turkey Tetrazzini, 186

Peach Cobbler Cake, 98

Pears
- Chopped or sliced, Apple-Pear Salad, 134

Peanuts, chopped, Caramel Apple Dip, 130

Pecans, chopped
- Bacon-Ranch Cheese Ball, 30
- Caramel Apple Dip, 130
- Crumb Coffee Cake, 162
- Easy Cheese Danish, 22
- Graham Cracker Toffee, 190

index — 205

Peach Cobbler Cake, 98
Pumpkin-Pecan Bread, 122
Potatoes
　Creamy Cheesy Potatoes, 182
　Loaded Baked Potato Soup, 178
Pumpkin
　Pumpkin Coffee Cake, 114
　Pumpkin-Pecan Bread, 122
　Pumpkin puree
　　Pumpkin Coffee Cake, 114
　　Pumpkin-Pecan Bread, 122

Q
Quick breads
　Cranberry Quick Bread, 158
　Pumpkin-Pecan Bread, 122

R
Ranch dressing mix, dry
　Bacon-Ranch Cheese Ball, 30
　Veggie Pizza, 70
　Loaded Baked Potato Dip, 126
　Stuffed Ranch Eggs, 78
Raspberries, fresh, in Berry Tarts, 74
Red kidney beans, canned, Secret Ingredient Chili, 142
Refreshing Fruit Salad, 34
Refried beans, 7-Layer Dip, 26
Refrigerated crescent rolls
　Easy Cheese Danish, 22
　Veggie Pizza, 70
Rice, cooked, Chicken Broccoli Rice Casserole, 42

S
Salads
　Apple-Pear Salad, 134
　Easy Cobb Salad, 38
　Salad greens, mixed
　　Apple-Pear Salad, 134
　　Easy Cobb Salad, 38
　　Refreshing Fruit Salad, 34
　　Strawberry Spinach Salad, 86
Salami or smoked sausage, Charcuterie Snack Board, 174
Secret Ingredient Chili, 142
Semisweet chocolate chips, Chocolate Chip Coconut Oatmeal Cookies, 146
Sweet pickle relish, Classic Potato Salad, 82
Soups
　Cream of chicken soup, condensed,
　　Chicken Broccoli Rice Casserole, 42
　Cream of mushroom soup, condensed,
　　Turkey Tetrazzini, 186
　Loaded Baked Potato Soup, 178
　Secret Ingredient Chili, 142
Sour cream
　Chicken Broccoli Rice Casserole, 42
　Corn Casserole, 138
　Creamy Cheesy Potatoes, 182
　Crumb Coffee Cake, 162
　7-Layer Dip, 26
　Loaded Baked Potato Dip, 126
　Loaded Baked Potato Soup, 178
　Taco Pasta Salad, 90
　Turkey Tetrazzini, 186
Spices
　Cayenne pepper, Million Dollar Dip, 170
　Chili powder, Secret Ingredient Chili, 142
　Cinnamon, ground
　　Apple Baked Oatmeal, 118
　　Apple-Cranberry Muffins, 166
　　Cranberry Quick Bread, 158
　　Crumb Coffee Cake, 162
　　Ginger Shortbread Cookies, 194
　　Mini Apple Bundt Cakes, 150
　　Peach Cobbler Cake, 98
　　Pumpkin Coffee Cake, 114
　　Pumpkin-Pecan Bread, 122
　Cloves, ground
　　Apple-Cranberry Muffins, 166
　Cumin, ground, Secret Ingredient Chili, 142
　Ginger, ground
　　Ginger Shortbread Cookies, 194
　　Pumpkin Coffee Cake, 114
　Garlic, minced
　　Secret Ingredient Chili, 142
　　Spinach-Artichoke Strata, 14
　Garlic powder
　　Bacon-Ranch Cheese Ball, 30
　　Chicken Broccoli Rice Casserole, 42
　　Creamy Cheesy Potatoes, 182
　　Million Dollar Dip, 170
　Nutmeg
　　Apple-Cranberry Muffins, 166
　　Ginger Shortbread Cookies, 194
　　Pumpkin-Pecan Bread, 122
　Paprika
　　Classic Potato Salad, 82
　　Million Dollar Dip, 170
　　Stuffed Ranch Eggs, 78

Sprinkles
  Ginger Shortbread Cookies, 194
  Chocolate Mint Brownies, 102
  Easy Patriotic Cookies, 94
  Marshmallow Pops, 198
Strawberries, fresh, see Fruit
Strawberry balsamic vinaigrette, Spinach Salad, 86
Sweetened condensed milk, Caramel Apple Dip, 130
Spinach-Artichoke Strata, 14
Strawberry Crinkle Cookies, 54
Strawberry Spinach Salad, 86
Stuffed Ranch Eggs, 78

T
Taco seasoning mix
  7-Layer Dip, 26
  Taco Pasta Salad, 90
Taco Pasta Salad, 90
Toffee bits
  Caramel Apple Dip, 130
  Graham Cracker Toffee, 190
Tomato sauce, Secret Ingredient Chili, 142
Turkey Tetrazzini, 186

V
Vegetables
  Artichoke hearts, canned, Spinach-Artichoke Strata, 14
  Baby spinach leaves
    Strawberry Spinach Salad, 86
    Spinach-Artichoke Strata, 14
  Broccoli, fresh, Veggie Pizza, 70
  Broccoli florets, frozen, Chicken Broccoli Rice Casserole, 42
  Carrots, Veggie Pizza, 70
  Celery ribs, Classic Potato Salad, 82
  Corn kernels, frozen, Taco Pasta Salad, 90
  Cucumber
    Veggie Pizza, 70
    Strawberry Spinach Salad, 86
  Green onions
    Bacon-Ranch Cheese Ball, 30
    7-Layer Dip, 26
    Loaded Baked Potato Dip, 126
    Loaded Baked Potato Soup, 178
    Million Dollar Dip, 170
    Veggie Pizza, 70
    Taco Pasta Salad, 90
  Lettuce
    Romaine
      Easy Cobb Salad, 38
      Strawberry Spinach Salad, 86
    Shredded, Taco Pasta Salad, 90
  Onion
    Classic Potato Salad, 82
    Turkey Tetrazzini, 186
    Secret Ingredient Chili, 142
    Spinach-Artichoke Strata, 14
  Red bell pepper
    Taco Pasta Salad, 90
    Spinach-Artichoke Strata, 14
  Red onion
    Apple-Pear Salad, 134
    Easy Cobb Salad, 38
    Strawberry Spinach Salad, 82
  Tomatoes
    7-Layer Dip, 26
    Veggie Pizza, 70
    Easy Cobb Salad, 38
    Taco Pasta Salad, 90
    Secret Ingredient Chili, 142
Vegetables, assorted, Charcuterie Snack Board, 134
Vanilla extract
  Berry Tarts, 74
  Blueberry Chip Muffins, 62
  Chocolate Chip Coconut Oatmeal Cookies, 146
  Easter Egg Blondies, 46
  Easy Cheese Danish, 22
  Graham Cracker Toffee, 190
  Ginger Shortbread Cookies, 194
  Mini Apple Bundt Cakes, 150

W
White chocolate chips, Blueberry Chip Muffins, 62

Dear Friend,

This book was prayerfully crafted with you, the reader, in mind. Every word, every sentence, every page was thoughtfully written, designed, and packaged to encourage you—right where you are this very moment. At DaySpring, our vision is to see every person experience the life-changing message of God's love. So, as we worked through rough drafts, design changes, edits, and details, we prayed for you to deeply experience His unfailing love, indescribable peace, and pure joy. It is our sincere hope that through these Truth-filled pages your heart will be blessed, knowing that God cares about you—your desires and disappointments, your challenges and dreams.

He knows. He cares. He loves you unconditionally.

BLESSINGS!

THE DAYSPRING BOOK TEAM

Additional copies of this book and
other DaySpring titles can be purchased
at fine retailers everywhere.
Order online at dayspring.com
or
by phone at 1-877-751-4347